Integrated Reporting and Corporate Governance

Corporate governance and corporate reporting are closely linked to each other, and their respective evolutionary patterns are mutually influencing. Along with the recent expansion of company disclosure, a growing attention is being paid to corporate governance determinants and mechanisms underpinning the decision to voluntarily adopt non-financial disclosure formats, such as integrated reporting.

At institutional level, several national corporate governance codes have been changed towards the recognition and inclusion of this innovative, non-financial language. In academic research, the influence of corporate governance variables vis-à-vis the choice to embrace such reporting practices has been subject to a long scrutiny. However, only a little inquiry has so far analysed the influence of corporate governance factors on integrated reporting adoption, quality, and credibility.

Accordingly, the aim of the book is to investigate if, and to what extent, corporate board composition and characteristics can affect, at the same time, the decision to voluntarily adopt integrated reporting by companies as well as their financial performance. The study carries out an empirical analysis of the professional features of board members at the time of their decision to implement integrated reporting as a new form of company accountability. The work provides innovative insights into the articulated relationships between the quantitative and qualitative composition of corporate boards and the latter's choice to uptake this advanced form of reporting to represent the wider value creation processes of their organisations.

Laura Girella (PhD, Ferrara) is a Researcher in Business Economics and Accounting at the University of Modena and Reggio Emilia (Italy), and a Technical and Research Manager at the International Integrated Reporting Council (IIRC). She is also a member of the Stakeholder Reporting Committee of the European Accounting Association (EAA).

Routledge Focus on Accounting and Auditing

Advances in the fields of accounting and auditing as areas of research and education, alongside shifts in the global economy, present a constantly shifting environment. This presents challenges for scholars and practitioners trying to keep up with the latest important insights in both theory and professional practice. Routledge Focus on Accounting and Auditing presents concise texts on key topics in the world of accounting research.

Individually, each title in the series provides coverage of a key topic in accounting and auditing, whilst collectively, the series forms a comprehensive collection across the discipline of accounting.

Gender and Corporate Governance
Francisco Bravo Urquiza and Nuria Reguera-Alvarado

Accounting, Representation and Responsibility
Deleuze and Guattarí Perspectives
Niels Joseph Lennon

Public Sector Audit
David C. Hay and Carolyn J. Cordery

Integrated Reporting and Corporate Governance
Boards, Long-Term Value Creation, and the New Accountability
Laura Girella

For more information about this series, please visit: www.routledge.com/Routledge-Focus-on-Accounting-and-Auditing/book-series/RFAA

Integrated Reporting and Corporate Governance

Boards, Long-Term Value Creation, and the New Accountability

Laura Girella

LONDON AND NEW YORK

First published 2021
by Routledge
2 Park Square, Milton Park, Abingdon, Oxon OX14 4RN

and by Routledge
52 Vanderbilt Avenue, New York, NY 10017

Routledge is an imprint of the Taylor & Francis Group, an informa business

British Library Cataloguing-in-Publication Data
A catalogue record for this book is available from the British Library

Library of Congress Cataloging-in-Publication Data
Names: Girella, Laura, author.
Title: Integrated reporting and corporate governance :
boards, long-term value creation, and the new
accountability / Laura Girella.
Description: Abingdon, Oxon ; New York, NY : Routledge,
2021. | Includes bibliographical references and index.
Identifiers: LCCN 2020045803 (print) | LCCN
2020045804 (ebook)
Subjects: LCSH: Corporate governance. | Boards of
directors. | Corporation reports. | Disclosure in accounting.
Classification: LCC HD2741 .G55 2021 (print) | LCC HD2741
(ebook) | DDC 658.15/12—dc23
LC record available at https://lccn.loc.gov/2020045803
LC ebook record available at https://lccn.loc.gov/2020045804

ISBN: 978-0-367-69371-8 (hbk)
ISBN: 978-1-003-14155-6 (ebk)

Typeset in Times New Roman
by codeMantra

to my children Alessandro, Alice and Giorgia Aurora and to my family

Contents

Illustrations

Figures

Tables

Foreword

Milton Friedman's doctrine (1970), which states that the only social responsibility of companies is to produce profits, has been overcome in
recent decades by increased attention to corporate governance issues
by shareholders, investment banks, and financial institutions, as well
as regulators and the general public as customers.

Boardrooms and governance professionals have been called upon
to give greater consideration to wider societal and environmental
concerns, as well as intangible considerations, resulting in renewed
time horizons for company evaluations and improved board attitudes,
decision-making, and performance.

This profound change in the role and objectives of corporate governance has transformed the concept of "value creation", which now
refers not only to the short but also to the medium and long terms and
covers the whole range of resources and relationships an organisation
uses and effects.

Integrated reporting is the most advanced and comprehensive in-
strument that boards and governance professionals can incorporate
into their strategy and business models to drive this expanded concept
of value creation, and test businesses resilience against factors such
as environmental, financial, and social capitals. To this end, the International Integrated Reporting Council (IIRC) has developed the
concept of *integrated thinking*, which not only constitutes the basis for
integrated reporting but also informs company management carried
out by boardroom members and executives.

Laura Girella's book addresses why, when, and how boards decide
to adopt integrated reporting, as they respond to new demands for
accountability, utilising the latest research, approaches, and methods.
It provides an important and timely insight into the composition and
characteristics of boards, with the increasingly varied backgrounds of

directors driving new viewpoints and providing the innovative mind-set needed for the adoption of integrated reporting.

With the exception of South Africa, integrated reporting is still a voluntary framework and yet increasing numbers of businesses are choosing to adopt it in countries around the world. It provides a tool to navigate the changing landscape in this post-Friedman era and is all the more relevant in an era of Covid-19.

Charles Tilley, OBE
Chief Executive Officer
International Integrated Reporting Council (IIRC)

Acknowledgments

I would like to thank Prof. Stefano Zambon for his continuing mentoring, advice, and motivation action.

I am also indebted to Mr. Mario Abela, World Business Council for Sustainable Development (WBCSD) for backing this project, and to Prof. Stefano Bonnini (University of Ferrara) for his invaluable statistical support.

Dr. Giuseppe Sudano has contributed to the preparatory work for this book.

I am very grateful to Mrs. Kristina Abbotts for her remarkable understanding and precious editorial assistance.

And finally, I am thankful to my partner and my kids for their lasting patience and emotional encouragement.

1   Introduction

> The company is an artificial person which has no heart, mind or soul of its own.
>
> Directors, once appointed, become the heart, mind and soul of the company.
>
> (Judge Professor Mervyn E. King, 2017)

The sense of the book

The aim of this book is to investigate if and to what extent corporate board composition and characteristics can affect, at the same time, the decision to voluntarily adopt integrated reporting by companies as well as their financial performance. These relationships are examined at the time of adoption and with reference to organisations located in countries other than South Africa, where this accountability tool is mandatory for listed companies.

Drawing on this analysis, the study intends to provide innovative insights into the articulated relationship between the quantitative and qualitative composition of corporate boards on the one side, and firm financial performance and the board's choice to uptake this advanced form of reporting on the other one.

Furthermore, the book also explores the association between the financial performance of the company and the decision of implementing integrated reporting. Some studies have in fact found the choice of integrated reporting as being guided by an "impression management" approach, i.e. as a means through which managers can favourably influence investors and stakeholders. Figure 1.1 summarises the linkages that will be explored in this study.

In this respect, this research can be located into the broader stream of academic and professional literature investigating the complex nexus of relationships between corporate governance determinants,

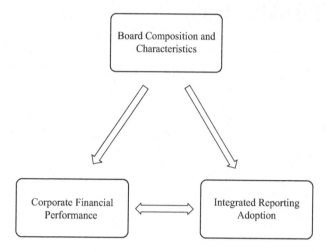

Figure 1.1 The linkages investigated in the book.

mechanisms, and consequences (De Villiers and Dimes, 2020), and, more specifically, it is sympathetic with the studies that have advanced that the human side of corporate governance and its linkage to value creation should be better understood (Huse, 2007).

In general terms, it can be said that corporate governance and corporate reporting are closely linked to each other, and their respective evolutionary paths appear to have been mutually influencing (Fiori and Tiscini, 2005; Kolk, 2008; Kolk and Pinkse, 2010; Chan et al., 2014).

From a theoretical viewpoint, since the emergence within companies of the separation between ownership and control (Berle and Means, 1932), conducive later to the Agency theory (Jensen and Meckling, 1976) and the doctrine of shareholder primacy and value (Rappaport, 1986), corporate governance has been mainly conceived as a way to guarantee investor protection. This view echoes the Milton Friedman's well-known philosophy on the basis of which the only social responsibility of corporations is to increase their profits for shareholders (Friedman, 1970).

In this respect, Shleifer and Vishny (1997, p. 737) state that "corporate governance deals with the ways in which suppliers of finance to corporations assure themselves of getting a return on their investment", while La Porta et al. (2000, p. 4) refer to corporate governance as a "set of mechanisms through which outside investors protect themselves against expropriation by the insiders", where 'the insiders' are embodied by managers and controlling shareholders. Hence, it can be maintained that Agency theory calls for a more significant proportion of outside and independent directors in the board, in that they can align more easily shareholder and manager interests, thus more effectively exerting the perceived board's primary function of 'control'. Interestingly enough, this modern view contrasts with the traditional vision going back to the 1930s, according to which the role of executives was instead to "instill the sense of moral purpose in company's employees" (Barnard, 1938, p. 89).

Only recently the various general calls for broadening the governance scope towards a more profound consideration of interests and needs of different categories of interests (Stakeholder theory) have started being heard (Freeman and Reed, 1983; Luoma and Goodstein, 1999). This approach has been essentially articulated in terms of corporate governance and board's behaviour through the Stewardship theory and the Resource-Dependence theory.

According to the Stewardship theory, managers are not only to be conceived as those to be controlled because they assume a self-interested and 'opportunistic behaviour'. They can have a 'good steward behaviour' (Donaldson and Davis, 1991, as they are moved by incentives that are not (only) of financial nature related to both their own satisfaction (i.e. recognition, personal achievement) and the organisational one (i.e. good performance or company success). It follows that the board's primary function is still that of control, but the latter is fundamentally shifted to managers, who thus become an integral component of the company's governing body. In other words, Stewardship theory favourably views the presence of insiders in the boardroom as, having a profound knowledge of the organisation, they can maximise shareholders' profit as well as outsiders' interests.

In addition to Agency and Stewardship conceptual approaches, Resource-Dependence theory has also been put forward to study corporate governance (Pfeffer and Salancik, 1978). The central focus of this theory expands beyond the needs and interests of providers of financial capital to consider the overall external environment in which the company operates. In particular, organisations aim to exert control on the surrounding context to assimilate the set of resources they need to survive. Accordingly, the function of the board of directors is not only that of acting as a monitoring body but also that of providing resources to the organisation through its external networks (Hillman and Dalziel, 2003).

On a broader perspective, there seems to be a wide consensus that over the years corporate governance and, consequently, board roles and functions have become more complex and difficult regarding not only the protection of the rights and interests of shareholders and investors, but more generally the response to the expectations of stakeholders, communities, and networks rotating around companies and their operations, and the information thereon (Huse and Rindova, 2001; Ayuso et al., 2014). This evolution has translated into various attempts to integrate the above delineated different theoretical views (Donaldson and Davis, 1991; Muth and Donaldson, 1998; Kiel and Nicholson, 2003; Nicholson and Kiel, 2007). In this respect, it might be interesting to consider whether also the relationship between board composition and its features, company financial performance, and integrated reporting can be better understood in light of a more unitary conceptual approach drawing on all of these diverse theories.

In parallel with the evolution of the roles of corporate governance, in the last 20 years corporate disclosure also has been relentless expanding its boundaries towards the enclosure of a more comprehensive set of information well beyond that required by financial reporting (Lev and Zarowin, 1999). At first, there has been the publication of information on the environmental and social impacts of organisational activities and then, more generally, on corporate value creation processes, also encompassing intangibles. This expansion process in company disclosure has been supported not only by a new political and societal climate and a relatively more open reporting attitude of companies, but also by innovative research findings, according to which disclosure of discretionary information should not be seen as necessarily negatively impacting firm performance and value (Verrecchia, 1983; Botosan, 1997).

In light of the above theoretical and practical developments, it is not surprising that the expansion of both the functions and roles of corporate governance on the one hand, and of voluntary disclosure, and in particular of reporting models other than the traditional financial one, on the other hand, has brought about a rising level of attention paid to the linkages between these two areas. In this picture, growing consideration is being given today to a better understanding of the corporate governance determinants that underlie the decision by corporate boards and managers to adopt and publish non-financial reporting formats. More and more, information about how this is organised influences perceptions and actions of companies. In this respect, the way in which organisations report externally on their activities and performance can be interpreted as the result of the mindsets and behaviours of those people who govern them, namely, the board members and the management team. Evidently, by implementing and communicating on their reports company's strategies, structures, and internal procedures, those people can also convey messages and diffuse an organisational culture that points to specific directions as opposed to others. Indeed, information and the way it is structured influence perceptions and actions in and around companies.

On the other hand, the relationship between corporate governance and reporting is not limited to an organisation's boundaries. External governance mechanisms, represented by institutional forces and national cultures, do play a role (La Porta et al., 2000; Duong et al., 2016). In this respect, it can be observed that national corporate governance Codes have also moved towards the recognition and inclusion of these new non-financial reporting languages and forms (see Chapter 2).

As to academic research, the influence of corporate governance mechanisms vis-à-vis the choice to embrace a given reporting practice has been subject to long scrutiny and debate. Many studies, based on differentiated theoretical approaches, have investigated the corporate governance features as explanatory factors of different types of disclosure, such as those relating to financial reporting, Corporate Social Responsibility (CSR), and Intellectual Capital (IC). However, only a few papers thus far have analysed the influence of corporate governance variables on the adoption of integrated reporting and the quality and credibility of this form of accountability. Even fewer studies have investigated this link in terms of board members' experience and background, even though different voices have recently advocated that also the diversification of the board is key for a balance between shareholder/stakeholder-ism, and namely long-term value creation (Barton, 2011; FCLT Global, 2019; Coffee, 2020) (for more depth, see Chapter 3). This perceived gap in the literature inspired the making of this book.

Within this frame, this introductory chapter intends to delineate some of the general issues associated with the relationship between voluntary disclosure and corporate governance, focussing on integrated reporting in the second part of this section.

Disclosure, voluntary disclosure, and corporate governance: some introductory remarks

Since the 1990s, an increasing interest in the issue of corporate disclosure has been manifested by legal systems, regulatory bodies, and investors. Following the financial scandals that occurred in the past

decades, the increased awareness of the relevance of corporate information for an efficient functioning of financial markets, as well as
the progressive articulation of the concept of value creation, has contributed to making the issue of corporate disclosure central (Benston
et al., 2004; Tiscini and Di Donato, 2006; Calder, 2008), also in its
voluntary dimension.

Several *factors* have contributed to this evolution. The core of corporate disclosure is of course based on the financial information required by national and international regulations and standards (i.e.
International Financial Reporting Standards (IFRS)), which results in
the periodic mandatory preparation of various corporate documents
(e.g. annual and quarterly-/half-year reports). However, as previously
delineated, company disclosure is no longer based only on what is required, but it also increasingly comprises information completing and
better illustrating the phenomena already reported on following laws
and standards. This information is commonly disclosed in financial
statements and the notes, the management commentary, the corporate governance statement, the compensation report, (sometimes) the
sustainability and/or the integrated report, and other operational and
institutional documents.

At the same time, the supranational dimension of the capital markets has placed in the foreground also the need to reach a greater
degree of homogeneity of corporate information regarding both the
structure and the contents of corporate documents to enhance the
understandability and comparability of financial data essential to
investment decision-making by current and potential investors in the
international arena.

Furthermore, it should be observed that the published annual reports are used today as a means for communicating both quantitative and qualitative corporate information not only to shareholders
and investors but also to all the other stakeholders. This situation has
led to a significant evolution in the contents of traditional mandatory
communication documents, especially in the case of listed companies.

As a further evolving factor of corporate disclosure, there is also
broad recognition of the importance of considering – along with all
stakeholder groups, particularly if they are heterogeneous –the va-
riety of institutional contexts and arrangements whose social values
are subject to change (Zajac and Westphal, 1994; Westphal and Zajac,
2001). This also applies to the need to communicate adequately –
covering not only legal compliance but also the institutional, social,
and organisational "fitting" – what is perceived to be good corporate
governance, which is, in turn, conditioned by the alternative interpretations of the various corporate actors (Hambrick et al., 2008).

Moreover, the orientation and scope of disclosure are influenced by the national cultural environment in which companies operate (Gray, 1988).

Another relevant factor is that information dissemination and processing have received increasing attention from companies around the world. This process is a consequence of the spreading of the new digitalised, knowledge-based economy, and the innovative digital tools and languages such as the XBRL (eXtensible Business Reporting Language).

Furthermore, a high-level disclosure could provide a more intense monitoring package to reduce opportunistic behaviour and information asymmetry (Li et al., 2008). Having said that, it is widely recognised, though, that financial reports do not reflect an extensive range of value creation activities relating to intangible assets (Lev and Zarowin, 1999). This deficiency gives rise to an increase in information asymmetries between businesses and users, and it allows for the creation of potential inefficiencies in the external resource allocation process. Indeed, numerous research reports (FASB, 2001; ASB, 2007) and academic studies (Lev, 2000; Mouritsen et al., 2001) have called for greater disclosure on intangibles and intellectual capital (Li et al., 2008).

Also voluntary non-financial disclosure, which began essentially with environmental reports in the 1980s and social accounts in the 1990s, has become widespread since then. Especially in the last decade, there has been an increasing adherence by companies to voluntary communication practices concerning corporate (governance structures, control systems, organisational climate, and well-being) and socio-environmental aspects (respect for human rights and the environment, human resource rights, company development, product safety, impact on society, communities, territories, and so on). The spreading of these practices has become even more frequent as a consequence of the growing changes taking place in the corporate operating environments and the pressure exerted by the different categories of stakeholders (Freeman, 1984; Carroll, 1991; Elijido-Ten et al., 2010; Fernandez-Feijoo et al., 2014). In this evolutionary context, in parallel to the voluntary diffusion of disclosure practices of non-financial information, this type of reporting has also been mandated for large companies in the European Union as a consequence of the European Directive no. 95/2014 (see below).

Looking more in depth at the corporate choice to proceed on with voluntary disclosure, it is rather evident that disclosure is the product of a management decision (Meek et al., 1995; Healy and Palepu, 2001). In general terms, the information gap existing between managers and shareholders/stakeholders generates information asymmetry. This phenomenon results from managers' private access to information about their efforts or beliefs, which are not observable by interested parties outside the company. Therefore, company transparency is a crucial factor for stakeholders, which will be able to determine an effective interaction between the latter and the company and its managers. Consequently, information asymmetry between a company's managers and stakeholders creates opportunities for voluntary disclosure decisions and actions to increase corporate transparency, and not only room for opportunistic behaviour by managers. Accordingly, the voluntary disclosure decision becomes a strategic response from the company to stakeholder expectations and information needs contrasting the information asymmetry phenomenon. On the other hand, voluntary disclosure can be a critical device capable of moderating the information asymmetry even between the different types of shareholders (Leuz and Verrecchia, 2000; Allegrini and Greco, 2013).

There are two fundamental types of voluntary disclosure. The first type occurs when a company decides on autonomous grounds to adopt, prepare, and disseminate disclosures following a regulation or a standard already in force and mandatory for other organisations, but that is not so for the company in question. Think of the national laws coming out from the implementation of the aforementioned Directive 2014/95/EU of the European Parliament and the European Council of 22 October 2014, amending Directive 2013/34/EU as regards the communication of non-financial information and the disclosure on the diversity from certain enterprises and large groups. For example, the legislative decree of 30 December 2016, no. 254, has implemented in Italy the provisions of that European Directive, making it mandatory for companies to disclose such information when they have a total of more than 500 employees during the financial year, and a consolidated balance sheet in which at least one of the following conditions is verified: total assets larger than 20 million euros or total net revenues from sales and services exceeding 40 million euros. There are several cases of Italian companies that, despite not being bound to follow the mandatory prescriptions of the decree no. 254/2016, they have decided spontaneously to publish the "Non-Financial Statement" regulated by that law. This type of voluntary disclosure can be labelled as "mimetic".

The second type of voluntary disclosure developed over the last 20 years or so, taking the form of spontaneous dissemination of data and information concerning corporate activity, which is additional to what is required by legislation. This type of disclosure has progressively emerged in relation to – and perhaps as a consequence of – the issuance by a plurality of public and private bodies of principles, standards, and reporting models on the social and environmental questions. Accordingly, this type of disclosure is based on non-mandatory sustainability standards that companies decide to follow spontaneously to reduce information asymmetries, improve their image, better understand and show how their value is actually generated, and many other reasons. That is why this category of voluntary disclosure can be referred to as "strategic non-imitative".

Probably, the most complete and advanced form of this second type of voluntary disclosure today is *integrated reporting* aimed to comprehend how a company creates value over time. The only country in the world where an integrated report cannot be considered a voluntary disclosure but has a mandatory nature is South Africa, where companies are required by the national corporate governance code (i.e. King Code IV) to prepare such form of reporting when they are listed on the Johannesburg Stock Exchange.

Research and surveys carried out on voluntary disclosure reveal the persistence of extreme heterogeneity in the practices currently adopted by companies, highlighting how the diffuse lack of detailed regulatory provisions and shared reporting models has led to the coexistence of different frameworks, tools, contents, and processes not only between different countries but also nationally (Boesso and Kumar, 2009; Leuz, 2010). More specifically, the empirical analyses developed on the topic have shown how the implementation of voluntary reporting and the forms and contents taken by it present a correlation with specific company characteristics such as its size, sector, and profitability, as well as the degree of market concentration.

In summary, it can be affirmed that over the last 10–20 years corporate disclosure has moved at an accelerated pace along two evolutionary paths: *from financial towards non-financial information, and from mandatory towards voluntary forms of reporting*. Corporate governance has played a fundamental role in both these shifts.

The emergence of integrated reporting and integrated thinking

Integrated reporting aims to tell the value creation story of a company by disclosing, in a concise manner, information on its corporate strategy, governance, risk management, performance, and prospects (IIRC, 2013).

Integrated reporting was launched by the International Integrated Reporting Committee (IIRC) in 2010. The first edition of the official

International Framework was published in December 2013. Integrated reporting functions as both a business management tool and a new external accountability vehicle, and it combines traditional financial reporting with sustainability performance and intangibles. It is a way to logically codify the reporting of corporate financial and non-financial information. The Framework of integrated reporting can be adopted not only by large companies as well as small- and medium-sized enterprises, but also by public sector entities and non-profit organisations. Integrated reporting provides a broader explanation of corporate performance than that shown by the traditional annual financial report (IIRC, 2013).

The IIRC is a global coalition made up of regulators, investors, companies, non-government organisations, and professionals operating in the accounting sector. The IIRC believes that communication on value creation is and should be the next step in the evolution of corporate reporting (IIRC, 2013). The long-term vision of the IIRC is a world in which integrated thinking is part of the main corporate practices of the public and private sectors, and which is facilitated by having integrated reporting as a corporate and corporate reporting norm. The cycle of integrated thinking and integrated reporting should act as a driver of financial stability and long-term sustainability by providing efficient and productive capital allocation. In the IIRC view, integrated reporting then aims to promote a more cohesive and efficient approach to corporate reporting and improve the quality of information communicated to financial capital suppliers, allowing them a more efficient and productive capital allocation. The IIRC perspective substantiates in a world in which the leading players in the business realm, public and private, think in an integrated way and are facilitated in this by using integrated reporting as their primary reporting tool.

Integrated reporting aims to improve the quality of the information provided to financial capital suppliers to allow them to pursue a more efficient and productive capital allocation. It also promotes a more cohesive and efficient approach to corporate reporting, by making it draw on different information elements while disclosing a wide range of factors that significantly affect an organisation's ability to produce value over time. Integrated reporting also pursues the goal to strengthen the accountability and responsibility of managing different forms of capital and guide the understanding of the interdependence between them, as well as supporting integrated thinking, decision-making, and corporate actions aimed at creating value in the short, medium, and long terms.

Although the integrated reporting process is consistent with the progress of financial and non-financial reporting, an integrated report differs from other forms of disclosure and communication in several respects. It focusses on an organisation's capacity to generate value in the short, medium, and long terms, and it enhances conciseness, strategic focus, orientation towards the future, and the connectivity of information and capitals, showing the mutual interdependencies.

An integrated report is closely linked to the concept of *integrated thinking*, which is the result of considering the relationships between the operational units and the functions of an organisation. It takes into account the connections and interdependencies between the numerous factors that influence an organisation's ability to create value, including the capitals that an organisation uses, the capability of an entity to respond to stakeholder needs, the ways in which an organisation adapts its business model and its strategy to respond to the external environment, and the elements that promote an entity's activities, performance, and results. The more an organisation can incorporate integrated thinking into its activities, the more natural it is to apply the concept of information connectivity in management reporting, analysis, and decision-making. This approach of integrated thinking also allows the information systems that support reporting activities and internal and external communication to be integrated more effectively. Hence, it can be said that it leads to an integrated decision-making process and actions aimed at creating value. In this respect, integrated thinking can be seen as a component of corporate governance in that it is a concept encouraging – primarily the board – to adopt an integrated approach to strategy and management, and thus the achievement of an ethical culture, a good performance, and effective control and legitimacy by an organisation (IODSA, 2016; Accountancy Europe, 2019). To put it differently, a sustainable success.

As stated in the International Framework (para. 1.8, p. 7, 2013), an integrated report is also meant to offer benefits to all stakeholders who are interested in an organisation's ability to create value over time, including employees, customers, suppliers, business partners, local communities, legislators, regulatory bodies, and policy-makers.

The Framework of integrated reporting adopts a principles-based approach. The aim is to achieve a balance between flexibility and the characterising features of integrated reporting, so to consider the many possible variations introduced by the specific circumstances regarding individual organisations and, at the same time, to reach a certain level of comparability between the disclosure of different organisations, which could be sufficient to meet the various needs for relevant information.

Integrated reporting must include, on a transitional basis and applying the "comply or explain" approach, also a declaration in which the members of the organisation's governance recognise their responsibility for the report.

An integrated report aims to provide detailed information on the resources used, called capitals, and the relationships on the basis of which an organisation generates value.

An integrated report is also intended to illustrate the ways in which an organisation interacts with the external environment and which are the capitals used to create value in the short, medium, and long terms. Capitals are value stocks that are increased, reduced, or transformed by an organisation's activities and outputs. Capitals are divided into six different types: financial, productive, intellectual, human, social and relational, and natural.

The ability of an organisation to create value for itself allows financial capital providers to realise an economic return. This ability is associated with the value created by the organisation for stakeholders and society in a broad sense through a wide range of activities, interactions, and relationships. When the latter significantly influence the ability to create value for the organisation itself, they are included in the integrated report.

An integrated report generally includes some ordinary contents that are closely related and can be presented simultaneously. They include the presentation of the organisation and the external environment; what the organisation does and in what circumstances it operates; how the organisation's governance structure supports its ability to create value over time; which is the organisation's business model; the specific opportunities and risks that affect the organisation's ability to create value and how they are managed; an evaluation of what the organisation's goals are and how it intends to achieve them; to what extent has the organisation achieved its strategic objectives and what are the achievements in terms of effects on capital; the challenges and uncertainties faced by the organisation in the implementation of its strategy; and the potential implications for its business model and future performance.

An organisation will determine the specific aspects to be included in its integrated report and how these aspects are quantified and evaluated. However, all this information must be contained in the integrated report to make it adequate and complete (IIRC, 2013). To claim that a reporting document is an integrated report, an explicit reference to the International IIRC Framework should be made.

The preparation of an integrated report must be based on some Guiding Principles, which include the following:

- Strategic focus and future orientation
- Connectivity of information
- Stakeholder relationship
- Materiality
- Conciseness
- Reliability
- Comparability

In addition to these principles, an integrated report is supposed to show the following Content Elements (IIRC, 2013):

- Organisational overview and external environment
- Governance
- Business model
- Risks and opportunities
- Strategy and resource allocation
- Performance
- Outlook

In summary, integrated report is a communication document that illustrates how an organisation's strategy, governance, performance, and perspectives allow it to create value in the short, medium, and long terms in the context in which it operates (IIRC, 2013).

Integrated reporting and corporate governance

After having introduced the relationship between corporate govern-ance and new forms of voluntary accountability, and having high-lighted integrated reporting as a new reporting practice able to respond to some of the information gaps of traditional financial reporting, one could wonder why organisations, and primarily the board, should de-vote resources and time to create such reporting form, i.e. the underly-ing reasons that can drive organisations to implement it.

Firms generally face higher demands for transparency and disclose information on key strategic decisions, which leads to request by ex-ternal parties for other types of information besides financial account-ing measures (Luo, 2005).

However, voluntary disclosure is not for free. As synthesised by Al-legrini and Greco (2013), companies wishing to reduce information asymmetries through disclosure may be affected by proprietary costs, litigation costs, and costs related to potential damage to existing financing relationships.

Since disclosure comes at a cost, companies could opt to strengthen internal control mechanisms instead of increasing the level of disclosure (Cheng and Courtenay, 2006; Cerbioni and Parbonetti, 2007). Similarly, businesses may prefer to reduce the costs associated with information asymmetries by improving corporate governance rather than increasing their level of disclosure.

In turn, the provision of voluntary disclosure generates specific costs for the organisation as well as benefits from the reduction in the amount of information asymmetry. The organisation's costs for this information include not only those linked to the processing and communication of information, but also the proprietary costs that could occur as a result of this information being used against the company by competitors, regulators, and other external pressure groups.

Despite the risks and costs that companies must bear to create an essentially voluntary disclosure such as an integrated report, this accountability practice is carried out voluntarily by many companies around the world (around 1,000 – cf. IIRC website), with the exception, as already stated, of the companies listed on the Johannesburg Stock Exchange, where it is mandatory in line with the King Code IV.

According to the traditional view of Milton Friedman (1970), based on liberalistic principles, businesses should only pursue profit while respecting laws and regulations, and this is the sole social responsibility they have. But at the same time, it is a reality that companies prepare these voluntary reports and information, incurring the related costs, which may seem to be a paradox.

As will be shown in Chapter 3, when analysing the academic literature, it emerges that the decision of adopting integrated reporting is dependent mainly on the corporate governance of a company. For example, Cheng et al. (2014) and Haji and Ghazali (2013) test the relationship between corporate governance and integrated reporting. They find that corporate governance plays a central role in the choice of preparing an integrated report within a company. On the other hand, Keenan and Aggestam (2001) argue that responsibility for the prudent investment in intellectual capital (which is one of the capitals considered in integrated reporting) lies with corporate governance, which must then structure – depending on the company – adequate processes for the communication of information on the value created for stakeholders through the intellectual capital of a company.

In this respect, the current corporate governance code of the companies listed on the Johannesburg Stock Exchange – the so-called King IV – states that corporate governance, and then company boards of directors, as well as integrated reporting are both essential to each other and have a very strong link. As recently stated by Professor Judge Mervyn E. King,

> the vision must be to have a company-centric governance model which moves away from yesterday's primacy of the shareholder. It needs to be implemented mindfully to achieve the four outcomes of effective leadership, value creation in a sustainable manner, adequate controls and legitimacy of operations. The International <IR> Framework is the light towards this goal.
>
> (2017)

Therefore, to understand why organisations spend time and invest continuously considerable resources in implementing integrated reporting, it is necessary to analyse which are the factors within the corporate governance that may affect the embracing of this accountability tool. In other terms, *what are the corporate governance variables, characteristics, and dynamics that are conducive to the decision to adopt an integrated report, despite the costs associated with it? Which is or are the theoretical frameworks that can better explain this relationship?*

Organisation of the book

The book is structured as follows. Chapter 2 provides an overview of how corporate governance Codes have been adapted worldwide in order to align and/or incorporate the principles of sustainability and integrated reporting. To do so, the analysis is based on those countries where corporate governance Codes have undergone a change towards the acknowledgement of integrated reporting. The main similarities and differences between those Codes are also outlined.

Chapter 3 is devoted to an examination of the major developments in academic and professional literature on the link between corporate governance and voluntary disclosure. More specifically, it analyses four main lines of enquiry, namely, corporate governance and voluntary disclosure, corporate governance and sustainability reporting, corporate governance and intellectual capital disclosure, and corporate governance and integrated reporting. The main similarities and differences between the four areas are outlined. Furthermore, on the basis of the literature review carried out, the hypotheses to be tested in the following session are developed.

In Chapter 4, the association between corporate governance and integrated reporting is illustrated through an empirical investigation. The analysis carried out rests on a statistical investigation aimed to understand to what extent the professional background of the members of the boards of directors can influence the voluntary adoption of this advanced reporting practice.

Finally, Chapter 5 summarises and critically examines the results obtained in previous chapters. It also discusses the conclusions that can be drawn in terms of theoretical and policy contributions and prospects for scholars and professionals researching and operating in these arenas.

Bibliography

Accountancy Europe (2019), *10 ideas to make corporate governance a driver of a sustainable economy.* Retrieved from https://www.accountancyeurope. eu/publications/10-ideas-to-make-corporate-governance-a-driver-of-a-sustainable-economy/.

Accounting Standards Board (ASB) (2007), *Review of Narrative Reporting by UK Listed Companies in 2006*, FRC. Retrieved from http://www.frc.org.uk/asb/press/pub1228.html.

Allegrini, M., and Greco, G. (2013), Corporate boards, audit committees and voluntary disclosure: Evidence from Italian listed companies. *Journal of Management & Governance, 17*(1), 187–216.

Ayuso, S., Rodríguez, M. A., García-Castro, R., and Ariño, M. A. (2014), Maximising stakeholders' interests: An empirical analysis of the stakeholder approach to corporate governance. *Business & Society, 53*(3), 414–439.

Barnard, Ch. (1938), *The function of the executive.* Cambridge, MA: Harvard University Press.

Barton, D. (2011), Capitalism for the long term, *Harvard Business Review*, March. Retrieved from https://hbr.org/2011/03/capitalism-for-the-long-term.

Benston, G., Bromwich, M., Litan, R. E., and Wagenhofer, A. (2004), *Following the money: The Enron failure and the state of corporate disclosure.* Washington, DC: Brookings Institution Press.

Berle, A., and Means, G. (1932), *The modern corporation and private property.* New York: Macmillan.

Boesso, G., and Kumar, K. (2009), An investigation of stakeholder prioritisation and engagement: Who or what really counts. *Journal of Accounting & Organizational Change, 5*(1), 62–80.

Botosan, C. A. (1997), Disclosure level and the cost of equity capital. *Accounting Review, 72*(3), 323–349.

Calder, A. (2008), *Corporate governance: A practical guide to the legal frameworks and international codes of practice*. Philadelphia, PA: Kogan Page.

Carroll, A. B. (1991), The pyramid of corporate social responsibility: Toward the moral management of organisational stakeholders. *Business Horizons, 34*(4), 39–48.

Chan, M. C., Watson, J., and Woodliff, D. (2014), Corporate governance quality and CSR disclosures. *Journal of Business Ethics, 125*(1), 59–73.

Cheng, E. C., and Courtenay, S. M. (2006), Board composition, regulatory regime and voluntary disclosure. *The International Journal of Accounting, 41*(3), 262–289.

Cheng, M., Green, W., Conradie, P., Konishi, N., and Romi, A. (2014), The international integrated reporting framework: Key issues and future research opportunities. *Journal of International Financial Management & Accounting, 25*(1), 90–119.

Coffee, John. C. Jr. (2020), Diversifying corporate boards — The best way toward a balanced shareholder/stakeholder system of corporate governance, *Promarket*, September 4th. Retrieved from https://promarket. org/2020/09/04/diversifying-corporate-boards-the-best-way-toward-a-balanced-shareholder-stakeholder-system-of-corporate-governance/.

De Villiers, C., and Dimes, R. (2020), Determinants, mechanisms and consequences of corporate governance reporting: A research framework. *Journal of Management and Governance*, 1–20.

Donaldson, L., and Davis, J. H. (1991), Stewardship theory or agency theory: CEO governance and shareholder returns. *Australian Journal of management, 16*(1), 49–64.

Duong, H. K., Kang, H., and Salter, S. B. (2016), National culture and corporate governance. *Journal of International Accounting Research, 15*(3), 67–96.

Fernandez-Feijoo, B., Romero, S., and Ruiz, S. (2014), Effect of stakeholders' pressure on transparency of sustainability reports within the GRI framework. *Journal of Business Ethics, 122*(1), 53–63.

Financial Accounting Standards Board (FASB) (2001), *Improving business reporting: Insights into enhancing voluntary disclosures*. Retrieved from https://www.fasb.org/news/nr012901.shtml.

Fiori, G., and Tiscini, R. (2005), Corporate governance, regolamentazione contabile e trasparenza dell'informativa aziendale [Corporate governance, accounting regulation and corporate information transparency]. Franco Angeli, Milan.

Focusing Capital on the Long Term (FCLT Global) (2019), *The long-term habits of a highly effective corporate board*. Retrieved from https://www.fcltglobal. org/resource/the-long-term-habits-of-a-highly-effective-corporate-board/.

Freeman, R. E. (1984), *Strategic management: A stakeholder perspective*. Englewood Cliffs, NJ: Prentice Hall.

Freeman, R. E., and Reed, D. L. (1983), Stockholders and stakeholders: A new perspective on corporate governance. *California Management Review, 25*(3), 88–106.

Friedman, M. (1970), The social responsibility of business is to increase its profits. *New York Times*, 13 September, p. 17.

Gray, S. J. (1988), Towards a theory of cultural influence on the development of accounting systems internationally. *Abacus, 24*(1), 1–15.

Haji, A. A., and Ghazali, N. A. M. (2013), A longitudinal examination of intellectual capital disclosures and corporate governance attributes in Malaysia, *Asian Review of Accounting, 21*(1), 27–52.

Hambrick, D. C., Werder, A. V., and Zajac, E. J. (2008), New directions in corporate governance research. *Organization Science, 19*(3), 381–385.

Healy, P. M., and Palepu, K. G. (2001), Information asymmetry, corporate disclosure, and the capital markets: A review of the empirical disclosure literature. *Journal of Accounting and Economics, 31*(1–3), 405–440.

Hillman, A. J., and Dalziel, T. (2003), Boards of directors and firm performance: Integrating agency and resource dependence perspectives. *Academy of Management Review, 28*(3), 383–396.

Huse, M. (2007), *Boards, governance and value creation: The human side of corporate governance*. Cambridge: Cambridge University Press.

Huse, M., and Rindova, V. P. (2001), Stakeholders' expectations of board roles: The case of subsidiary boards. *Journal of Management and Governance, 5*(2), 153–178.

Institute of Directors of South Africa (IODSA) (2016), King IV report on corporate governance for South Africa. Retrieved from https://cdn.ymaws.com/www.iodsa.co.za/resource/collection/684B68A7-B768-465C-8214-3A007F15A 5A/IoDSAKing_IV_Report-WebVersion.pdf.

International Integrated Reporting Council (IIRC) (2013), *International <IR> Framework*. Retrieved from https://integratedreporting.org/resource/international-ir-framework/.

Jensen, M. C., and Meckling, W. H. (1976), Theory of the firm: Managerial behavior, agency costs and ownership structure. *Journal of Financial Economics, 3*(4), 305–360.

Keenan, J., and Aggestam, M. (2001), Corporate governance and intellectual capital: Some conceptualisations. *Corporate Governance: An International Review, 9*(4), 259–275.

Kiel, G. C., and Nicholson, G. J. (2003), Board composition and corporate performance: How the Australian experience informs contrasting theories of corporate governance. *Corporate Governance: An International Review, 11*(3), 189–205.

King, M. E. (2017), Keynote address by Judge Professor Mervyn King at the Integrated Reporting Committee of South Africa Conference' three board agenda items for the 21st century', 27 July 2017.

Kolk, A. (2008). Sustainability, accountability and corporate governance: Exploring multinationals' reporting practices. *Business Strategy and the Environment, 17*(1), 1–15.

Kolk, A., and Pinkse, J. (2010). The integration of corporate governance in corporate social responsibility disclosures. *Corporate Social Responsibility and Environmental Management, 17*(1), 15–26.

La Porta, R., Lopez-de-Silanes, F., Shleifer, A., and Vishny, R. (2000), Investor protection and corporate governance. *Journal of Financial Economics, 58*(1–2), 3–27.

Leuz, C. (2010), Different approaches to corporate reporting regulation: How jurisdictions differ and why. *Accounting and Business Research, 40*(3), 229–256.

Leuz, C., and Verrecchia, R. E. (2000), The economic consequences of increased disclosure. *Journal of Accounting Research, 38*, 91–124.

Lev, B. (2000), *Intangibles: Management, measurement, and reporting.* Washington, DC: Brookings Institution Press.

Lev, B., and Zarowin, P. (1999), The boundaries of financial reporting and how to extend them. *Journal of Accounting Research, 37*(2), 353–385.

Li, J., Pike, R., & Haniffa, R. (2008), Intellectual capital disclosure and corporate governance structure in UK firms. *Accounting and Business Research, 38*(2), 137–159.

Luo, Y. (2005), Corporate governance and accountability in multinational enterprises: Concepts and agenda. *Journal of International Management, 11*(1), 1–18.

Luoma, P., and Goodstein, J. (1999), Stakeholders and corporate boards: Institutional influences on board composition and structure. *Academy of Management Journal, 42*(5), 553–563.

Meek, G. K., Roberts, C. B., and Gray, S. J. (1995), Factors influencing voluntary annual report disclosures by US, UK and continental European multinational corporations. *Journal of International Business Studies, 26*(3), 555–572.

Mouritsen, J., Larsen, H. T., and Bukh, P. N. (2001), Intellectual capital and the 'capable firm': Narrating, visualising and numbering for managing knowledge. *Accounting, Organisations and Society, 26*(7–8), 735–762.

Muth, M., and Donaldson, L. (1998), Stewardship theory and board structure: A contingency approach. *Corporate Governance: An International Review, 6*(1), 5–28.

Nicholson, G. J., and Kiel, G. C. (2007), Can directors impact performance? A case-based test of three theories of corporate governance. *Corporate Governance: An International Review, 15*(4), 585–608.

Pfeffer, J., and Salancik, G. R. (1978), *The external control of organisations: A resource dependence perspective.* New York: Harper & Row.

Rappaport, A. (1986), *Creating shareholder value: The new standard for business performance.* New York: Free Press.

Shleifer, A., and Vishny, R. W. (1997), A survey of corporate governance. *The Journal of Finance, 52*(2), 737–783.

Tiscini, R., and Di Donato, F. (2006), The relation between accounting frauds and corporate governance systems: An analysis of recent scandals. Retrieved from https://papers.ssrn.com/sol3/papers.cfm?abstract-id=1086624.

Verrecchia, R. E. (1983), Discretionary disclosure. *Journal of Accounting and Economics, 5,* 179–194.

Westphal, J. D., and Zajac, E. J. (2001), Decoupling policy from practice: The case of stock repurchase programs. *Administrative Science Quarterly, 46*(2), 202–228.

Zajac, E. J., and Westphal, J. D. (1994), The costs and benefits of managerial incentives and monitoring in large US corporations: When is more not better?. *Strategic Management Journal, 15*(S1), 121–142.

2 Corporate governance and integrated reporting

An international perspective

As previously mentioned, corporate governance and disclosure are two elements that go hand-in-hand. This linkage can find its premises both at a firm level and at an institutional level. Companies may decide to change their governance structure and disclosure practices not only to better align to their *raison d' être* (profit vs. shared value), but also to respond to the normative or legitimacy forces deriving from the environment in which they operate.

Accordingly, this chapter will provide an overview of how corporate governance Codes have been adapted worldwide to align and/or incorporate the principles of this new form of long-term accountability tool, namely, integrated reporting. To do so, the analysis will be based on a chronological examination of those countries where corporate governance Codes have undergone a change towards the acknowledgement of integrated reporting. The common denominators that characterise this process will be outlined at the end of this chapter.

South Africa: the King Code experience

South Africa is probably the most well-known example of a country that has witnessed a radical change in corporate behaviour, thanks to the inclusion of recommendations of reporting practices into governance principles. This evolution started in 1993, few years after the end of the Apartheid, when the Institute of Directors in Southern Africa (IoDSA) asked Prof. Judge Mervyn E. King to chair a Committee on corporate governance in order to restore good governance practices in the country. During the Apartheid era, South Africa became, in fact, isolated from the global economy and companies, not being subject to foreign competition, had no greater incentive to adopt sound corporate governance practices able to protect their investors and stakeholders in general. Only when the African National Congress won the election in 1994, and Nelson Mandela was appointed President, firms felt under pressure. In addition to Prof. King, the Committee was composed of Philip Armstrong, Nigel Payne, and Richard Wilkinson, three well-known experts in the field of corporate governance in South Africa.

After one year of work, in 1994, the Committee issued the first version of the Report, which then became known as 'King Report' (IODSA, 1994). It represented the first corporate governance code for the South African context. It addressed companies listed on the Johannesburg Stock Exchange, and other large organisations, such as public entities as defined by the Public Entities Act of South Africa, banks, financial, and insurance companies as defined by the Financial Services Acts of South Africa, and large unlisted companies. The originality of this document relied not only on being the first in the region but most importantly on its structure and contents. Differently from Codes in other countries, it did not have regulatory power and, as such, it was based on principles (at least until 2016). Furthermore, it adopted a 'comply or explain' approach, which was almost unique internationally. In terms of contents, the main principles covered aspects such as the definition of the composition and the mandate of the board of directors and, specifically, the characteristics that non-executive directors should possess as well as the rules that should guide their appointments to the board and some guidance on the maximum term for executive directors. It also included principles about the determination and disclosure of executive and non-executive directors' remuneration, the frequency of board meetings, the requirement for effective auditing, the presence of an affirmative action programme included in the business plan, and the implementation of the Code of ethics. Its main innovative spirit was related to the indication that the board is responsible for the issuance of a balanced annual report and, in general, of transparent communications able to take into consideration the demands by the society for "greater transparency and accountability from corporations regarding their non-financial affairs". Hence, the request was for a report to "address material matters of significant interest and concern to all stakeholders" (Chapter 20). It can then be stated that the first version of the King Report adopted a stakeholder approach to corporate governance. It was important to regulate the relationship between directors, shareholders, and stakeholders in a moment where the control of companies was shifting from families to institutions (IODSA, King I, 1994, p. 1).

Quite soon, in 2002, King Report I underwent a revision (IODSA, 2002). Its target audience was enlarged to financial institutions, public sector companies, and agencies included in the Public Finance Management Act of South Africa and the Johannesburg Stock Exchange required listed companies to comply with the Code or to provide reasons for non-compliance. Its contents broadened towards the inclusion of an ad hoc section on sustainability, the role of the board, and risk management. More specifically, it introduced the concept of 'integrated sustainability reporting' which encompasses the inclusion of a wider set of non-financial information. In other words, companies were encouraged to prepare a sustainability report in addition to annual financial accounts, and the board was deemed responsible towards all stakeholders. King II states:

> Successful governance in the world of the 21st century requires companies to adopt an inclusive and not an exclusive approach. The company must be open to institutional activism and there must be greater emphasis on the sustainable or non-financial aspects of its performance. Boards must apply the test of fairness, accountability, responsibility and transparency in all acts or omissions and be accountable to the company but responsive and responsible towards the company's identified stakeholders. The correct balance between conformance with governance principles and performance within an entrepreneurial market economy must be found, but this will be specific to each company.
>
> (IODSA, King II, 2002, p. 20)

In light of the changes that were occurring at a national and international level, especially as a result of the IT advances, in 2009 a new version of the Code, the King Code III, was released (IODSA, 2009). The most significant change related to the fact that companies were not asked to produce a sustainability report *in addition to* a financial report anymore, but to integrate information on governance, strategy, and sustainability. It first introduced the concept of 'integrated annual reporting' defined as "a holistic and integrated representation of the company's performance in terms of both its finances and sustainability". As pointed out by Mervyn King (2009, p. 14)

> the board should take into consideration four capitals, namely financial capital which is provided by shareholders, human capital by employees, natural capital by natural resources, such as air, water and land and social capital by the actors surrounding companies activities.

In terms of adoption, the Code became applicable to all entities (SMEs included), with an 'apply or explain' approach. This was to avoid situations of non-compliance by private companies that became recurrent in the country. In fact, they did not look at King II as being applicable to them, but this did not correspond with the primary objective of the King Codes to ensure good governance principles to be adopted by all South African companies.

In 2016, the final version of the King Code, the King Code IV, was published (IODSA, 2016). Despite the fact that it retained most of the contents of the King Code III, even though on a reduced basis (from 75 to 17 principles, with the 17 ones being applicable only to institutional investors) and that it included recommended practices instead of principles, some significant differences are present between the two versions. First, King IV moved from the initial approach of 'apply or explain' to that of 'apply and explain', this meaning that the board should report on the recommended practices that have been adopted, on how they have been implemented, and on which ones will be uptaken in the coming financial year. Second, it introduced additional sector supplements to support municipalities, non-profit organisations, retirement funds, small- and medium-sized enterprises, and state-owned entities to interpret better and apply the recommendations. Furthermore, while information technology was recognised as one source of value creation in the King Code III, the King Code IV separates information from technology. It also, most importantly, stresses the concept of *'outcomes-based' corporate governance* to ensure internal and external stakeholders could come to the conclusion that the company, in the person of the high governing body, has been practising good corporate governance (King and Ajogwu, 2020). The King Code IV introduced also an outcomes-based report, i.e. the integrated reporting, which relies on a multi-capital view of the value creation process, where inputs are transformed into outputs through company activities and are transferred into the society as outcomes. In the same version of the Code, the UN Sustainable Development Goals (SDGs), being outcomes-based, have also been included.

The King Committee hence started discussing what should be the outcomes of governance and agreed on four of them, namely, value creation (in a sustainable manner), ethical culture with effective leadership (meaning that directors are responsible for the company), adequate and effective internal controls (the board has an informed oversight of the management), and trust and confidence of the community in which the company operates.

Japan

Japan has been a pioneer, together with South Africa, in revisiting its corporate governance practices towards the inclusion of the principles of integrated reporting. After the 2008 financial crisis that hit the worldwide economy, Japan also felt the need to revitalise its economy. Hence, at the end of 2012, the government established the Headquarters for Japan's Economic Revitalization within the Cabinet with the aim to formulate policy strategies able to reinvigorate the economic system. As part of this project, approved in June 2013, the principles for institutional investors to fulfil their fiduciary responsibilities have also been discussed. The Financial Services Agency established then the Council of Experts Concerning the Japanese Version of the Stewardship Code which in 2014 released the Japan Stewardship Code. The main aim of this Code was to set principles that institutional investors and fund managers (that invest in Japanese listed shares) could adhere to – on a voluntary basis – to fulfil their stewardship responsibilities defined as "the responsibilities of institutional investors to enhance the medium to long term investment return for their clients and beneficiaries" (p. 1). Similarly to the King Code, it adopts a principles-based and a 'comply or explain' approach. It is based on seven principles, two of which are clearly aligned to integrated reporting. Principle 3 affirms that "institutional investors should monitor investee companies so that they can appropriately fulfil their stewardship responsibilities with an orientation towards the sustainable growth of the companies", while Principle 7 states that

> To contribute positively to the sustainable growth of investee companies, institutional investors should have in-depth knowledge of the investee companies and their business environment and skills and resources needed to appropriately engage with the companies and make proper judgments in fulfilling their stewardship activities.
>
> (p. 6)

Although not explicitly mentioned, integrated reporting can thus represent for Japanese institutional investors a useful vehicle through which they can follow these principles in that it tells the value creation story of companies by taking into consideration their strategies, governance, performances based on six capitals and prospects. The Code has been recently revised in 2017 by including a guidance on the role of assets managers.

In addition to the Stewardship Code, in 2015 another fundamental document made its first appearance on the Japanese corporate governance scene, the Corporate Governance Code. The Code has always been conceived in the remit of the Japan Revitalization Strategy to enhance corporate governance practices in the country. It has been elaborated by the Council of Experts Concerning the Corporate Governance Code with the Financial Services Agency and the Tokyo Stock Exchange serving as joint secretariat.

It contains five General Principles, each of which is articulated in Principles and Supplementary Principles, and it adopts a principles-based, 'comply or explain' approach. Two of the Guiding Principles can be of particular interest to integrated reporting – even though the entire philosophy informing the document appears quite close to that of integrated reporting in that it refers to corporate governance as "a structure for transparent, fair, timely and decisive decision-making by companies, with due attention to the needs and perspectives of shareholders and also customers, employees and local communities" (p. 1). According to Principle 3,

> Companies should appropriately make information disclosure in compliance with the relevant laws and regulations, but should also strive to actively provide information beyond that required by law. This includes both financial information, such as financial standing and operating results, and non-financial information, such as business strategies and business issues, risk, and governance. The board should recognise that disclosed information will serve as the basis for constructive dialogue with shareholders, and therefore ensure that such information, particularly non-financial information, is accurate, clear and useful.
>
> (p. 2)

Hence, this principle moved into the direction of encouraging companies to disclose information beyond that of financial nature, because this can facilitate the relationship with shareholders. It is in line with the logic of an integrated report, according to which value is created primarily for the organisation, and thus shareholders, in order to inform decision-making, and then, for the other stakeholders.

> The importance of creating a dialogue with shareholders is also reinforced in Principles 5 which states that "in order to contribute to sustainable growth and the increase of corporate value over

the mid- to long-term, companies should engage in constructive dialogue with shareholders even outside the general shareholder meeting".

(p. 3)

Similarly to Principle 3, providers of financial capital are seen as contributing, in a constructive manner, to the value creation process of an organisation.

Finally, in 2017 the Ministry of Economy, Trade and Industry (METI) released the Corporate Governance System Practical Guidelines (CGS Guidelines), which are aimed to support companies in applying corporate governance principles. In 2018, the Corporate Governance Code has been reviewed, and the Financial Services Agency has finalised the Guidelines for Investor and Company Engagement, which are meant to supplement both the Corporate Governance Code and the Stewardship Code, by encouraging both institutional investors and companies to implement both Codes. In the same year, METI announced some revisions to the Corporate Governance System Practical Guidelines. In March 2020, the Stewardship Code has also been reviewed (after that the Expert Council called for it). The key change asks institutional investors and fund managers to take into consideration the Environmental, Social and Governance (ESG)factors in their engagements in a medium and long perspective.

India

In June 2017, the Securities and Exchange Board of India (SEBI), i.e. the non-statutory body that regulates the securities market, established a multi-stakeholder Committee on Corporate Governance (the so-called "Kotak Committee") aiming to enhance the standards of corporate governance of listed companies in the country. Among other issues, the Committee was deemed to provide SEBI with recommendations regarding "disclosure and transparency-related issues, with any" (Press Release no. 60/2017). This step followed of a few months a Circular by the same body that encouraged the top 500 listed companies in India to adopt integrated reporting in line with the International Organization of Securities Commissions (IOSCO)principles of disclosure of material information to investors. In particular, the Circular asked the 500 companies that are required to prepare a Business Responsibility Report (BRR) to voluntarily implement integrated reporting from the financial year 2017 to 2018, rather than only a sustainability report, by including this information in the annual report in a separate section, or by incorporating it in the Management Discussion & Analysis, or by preparing a separate integrated report (Circular, February 2017). In the case in which the information in accordance with integrated reporting is not contained in the annual report, it can be published on the company's website and referenced.

The Business Responsibility Report, now called Business Responsibility and Sustainability Report, is a document that has been made mandatory by SEBI for the top 100 listed entities in 2012, and then extended to the top 500 in 2015 and the top 1,000 in 2019 based on their market capitalisation. It originally emanated from the *National Voluntary Guidelines on Social, Environmental and Economic Responsibilities of Business* (NVGs) released in 2011 by the Ministry of Corporate Affairs, Government of India, to provide guidance to businesses on what is responsible business conduct. The Guidelines have been reviewed in 2018 and released under the new name *National Guidelines on Responsible Business Conduct* (NGRBC) in 2019. The Business Responsibility and Sustainability Report requires companies to report information on their non-financial impacts, such as that on the environment, the respect of human rights, and the stakeholder relationships.

Malaysia

Concurrently with the Indian example, in 2017 the Securities Commission of Malaysia has released the third version of the Malaysian Code on Corporate Governance (MCCG), according to which large companies are called to adopt integrated reporting based on the International <IR> Framework. More specifically, in Principle C on *Integrity in Corporate Reporting and Meaningful Relationship with Stakeholders*, Guidance 11.2, an integrated report is defined as "the main report from which all other detailed information flows, such as annual financial statements, governance, and sustainability reports" (p. 46). Hence, the integrated report is seen as a means through which the organisation, and specifically the board, establishes good relationships with stakeholders. This step follows the adoption by listed companies in the country of some of the elements contained in the integrated report, which include a better link between performance and strategy and in general a better definition of the strategic priorities. Despite the above most of the firms still conceive corporate reporting as a compliance exercise, even though an improvement in the quality of the reports has been noticed (PwC, 2018). Furthermore, the MCCG increased board responsibilities towards the inclusion of the management in the preparation of the integrated report, the delegation of monitoring activities to ad hoc committees that should frequently monitor the process and the identification of strategic guidelines.

The UK

In July 2018, the UK Corporate Governance Code has also undergone a revision together with the Guidance on Board Effectiveness. The new version of the Code issued by the Financial Reporting Council (FRC) (2018) broadens the definition of governance by emphasising the importance of stakeholder relationships, a clear purpose and strategy for companies in alignment with a healthy corporate culture, a high quality of the board with a focus on diversity, and a remuneration which should be proportionate and support long-term success. In specific regards to stakeholder relationships, Principle 1D calls for the board to ensure effective engagement and encourages participation from both shareholders and stakeholders. In particular, it calls on directors to "describe in their annual report how the interests of a wide stakeholder community as set out in section 172 of the Companies Act have been considered in board discussions and decision-making" (Provision 5, p. 5). This way, it aligns to the view set out in the International <IR> Framework, which states that the report should disclose information on how stakeholders' needs and interests have been taken into consideration and dealt with.

Provision 1 relating to Principle 1A-E underlines the board's responsibility to "assess the basis on which the company generates and preserves value over the long-term" and describes "the sustainability of the company's business model and how its governance contributes to the delivery of its strategy" (p. 4). Thus, it implicitly refers to some of the critical aspects of an integrated report, namely, the focus on the long-term view of value creation and the centrality of the business model and governance to ensure the achievement of the organisational strategy.

Finally, the new UK Code emphasises the need for wider connectivity between the information contained in the corporate governance report and in other parts of the annual report to improve the decision-making of shareholders. It affirms that corporate governance reporting should "relate coherently to other parts of the annual report – particularly the Strategic Report and other complementary information – so that shareholders can effectively assess the quality of the company's corporate governance activities" (p. 3). In so doing, it aligns to the principle of connectivity included in the IIRC Framework, which refers to the interdependencies that exist between the different set of qualitative and quantitative information, the capitals and the short-, medium-, and long-term performance of a company.

Australia

As compared to other countries, in Australia the alignment of the corporate governance code with the principles of integrated reporting has occurred relatively recently, i.e. in 2019, but coming into force for financial years commencing on, or after, 1 January 2020. However, the approach undertaken has been quite robust. Probably, the most significant changes are related to: (a) the substitution of the term 'social license to operate' with the expressions 'reputation' and 'standing in the community', and (b) the expansion of boards' responsibilities.

As to the first aspect, it is interesting to note that it originated from the willingness of the ASX (Australian Stock Exchange) Corporate Governance Council to render the concept of 'social licence to operate' more understandable (2019). In commenting on this shift, the Council has in fact maintained that, while the terms 'social license to operate' and 'reputation' and 'standing in the community' have to be considered as synonymous, the latter is "more likely to be better understood and more consistently applied by listed entities, their boards and other stakeholders" (Financial Review, 2019). Principle 3, Recommendation 3.1, now reads

> in formulating its values, a listed entity should consider what behaviours are needed from its officers and employees to build long term sustainable value for its security holders. This includes the need for the entity to preserve and protect its reputation and standing in the community and with key stakeholders, such as customers, employees, suppliers, creditors, law makers and regulators.
>
> (p. 16)

This appears to be consistent with the <IR> Framework Guiding Principle on 'stakeholder relationship', which calls for the importance for the organisation to take into consideration and respond to the needs and interests of stakeholders and, more in general, with the idea that an organisation creates value for itself and the others (International <IR> Framework, pp. 10–11, 17–18).

As to the second aspect, the board is asked to assume responsibility for a new number of issues, such as defining organisational purpose, ensuring alignment between remuneration policies and the entity's purpose, values, strategic objectives, and risk appetite and a stronger focus on the role of the board in overseeing management and, where necessary, also challenging management. Principle 4, and Recommendation 4.3 in particular, makes it clear that the board is responsible for the processes used to verify the integrity of all 'periodic corporate reports', and it states explicitly that the principles of integrated reporting can be used in preparing existing reports, including the Operating & Financial Review (OFR) (p. 20).

Furthermore, Principle 7 refers to the importance to the board to establish a sound risk management framework. The Commentary to Recommendation 7.2 asks the board to ensure that the risk management framework deals with emerging risks, and specifically sustainability and climate change risks (p. 27). Integrated reporting forms a part also of Recommendation 7.4 of the Code – in addition to Recommendation 4.3 – which looks at disclosure on environmental and social risks and how an entity plans to manage such risks. It maintains

> how an entity manages environmental and social risks can affect its ability to create long-term value [...] To make the disclosures called for under this recommendation does not require a listed entity to publish an "integrated report" or "sustainability report". However, an entity that does publish an integrated report in accordance with the IIRC International <IR> Framework, or a sustainability report in accordance to a recognised international standard, may meet this recommendation simply by cross-referring to that report.
>
> (p. 27)

From the above, it can be drawn that integrated report is conceived as a way for the board to better monitor the integrity of corporate disclosure and the management of a wide range of risks.

Italy

In Italy, the Corporate Governance Code cannot be considered as one of those that have already aligned to integrated reporting. Rather, it could be said that this country is on its journey towards it. This journey started a couple of years ago, i.e. in 2018, when the word 'sustainability' appeared for the first time among the criteria regarding the stated role of the board of directors, and in particular the definition of the risk profile of the company (Borsa Italiana Corporate Governance Committee, 2018). In the 2020 version of the Code, a more explicit approach has been undertaken, and the expression 'sustainable success' has directly entered among the responsibilities of the board of directors Borsa Italiana Corporate Governance Committee, 2020). It is indeed possible to read "The board of directors leads the company by pursuing its sustainable success. [...] The board of directors promotes dialogue with shareholders and other stakeholders which are relevant for the company, in the most appropriate way" (Corporate Governance Code, 2020, p. 5).

Another new element introduced by the 2020 Code is the analysis of the influence of sustainability on dialogue and involvement activities between the companies and their stakeholders. The relationship that the companies must have with investors, especially of an institutional nature, acquires distinct relevance in the Code, where Recommendation 3 specifies that the board should adopt specific policies of engagement. These policies have to respond to the continuous request by investors for discussion on both the conduct of the business and the corporate governance structures. In this regard, the Code entrusts the Chairman of the board with the two tasks of proposing to the entire administrative body, together with the CEO, the implementation of a specific engagement policy, and of ensuring that the board itself is promptly informed of its contents.

In order to stress the relevance of the concept of sustainability, the new 2020 Code also intervened on the remuneration policies of directors, the members of the corporate control body, and the top management. It is specified that the task of the board of directors is also to establish, assisted by the Remuneration Committee, a remuneration policy aimed at pursuing the sustainable success of the company. In particular, it should be noted that a significant part of this specific policy must be linked to long-term performance objectives.

As to the internal control and risk management system, while in the 2018 version the word 'sustainability' was included in the criteria, in the 2020 edition it is comprised directly in the principles. In this sense, the board, assisted by an ad hoc committee, is called to be responsible for integrating sustainability objectives into the preparation of the industrial plan of the company and/or the group it heads.

Conclusion

The chapter had the aim to offer a review of those national corporate governance Codes that have included or started aligning their principles to those of integrated reporting. In particular, the cases of South Africa, Japan, India, the UK, Malaysia, Australia, and Italy have been illustrated.

In this respect, it has been described how the South Africa case represents a unique example in that integrated reporting is mandatory for listed companies.

From the analysis conducted, it appears clear that, although different paths and ways have been followed to achieve this goal, some common features can be detected. More specifically, it can be noted that three are the fundamental principles that have been most commonly aligned with, or included in, the different Corporate Governance Codes, namely the 'stakeholder relationships', the 'risks and opportunities' and the 'value creation'. The importance to the board to take into consideration stakeholders' voices has guided this process of alignment in Australia, Japan, Malaysia, and the UK. Put it differently, in all the four countries the principles of integrated reporting have been conceived as a vehicle through which the organisation, and especially the board, could be able to better engage with both shareholders and stakeholders. The new Australian Corporate Governance Code has also referred expressly to the integrated reporting principles in order to rely on a sound risk management approach. Finally, both the UK and Japanese Corporate Governance Codes have now encompassed a conceptualisation of value, which is consistent with that characterising integrated reporting, i.e. value has to be created for the organisation and for the others and adopting a medium- and long-term perspective.

Bibliography

ASX Corporate Governance Council (2019), *Corporate governance principles and recommendations* (4th Edition). Retrieved from https://www.asx.com.au/regulation/corporate-governance-council.htm.

Borsa Italiana Corporate Governance Committee (2018), *Corporate governance code.* Retrieved from https://www.borsaitaliana.it/comitato-corporate-governance/homepage/homepage.en.htm.

Borsa Italiana Corporate Governance Committee (2020), *Corporate governance code.* Retrieved from https://www.borsaitaliana.it/comitato-corporate-governance/homepage/homepage.en.htm.

Financial Reporting Council (2018), *The UK Corporate governance code.*

Financial Review (2019), ASX governance council dumps 'social licence to operate' from guidance. Retrieved from https://www.afr.com/work-and-careers/management/asx-governance-council-dumps-social-licence-to-operate-from-guidance-20190225-h1bp43.

Institute of Directors of South Africa (IODSA) (1994), *King report on corporate governance for South Africa.* Parktown, November.

Institute of Directors of South Africa (IODSA) (2002), *King report on corporate governance for South Africa*. Parktown, March.

Institute of Directors of South Africa (IODSA) (2009), *King report on corporate governance for South Africa*. Parktown, September.

Institute of Directors of South Africa (IODSA) (2016), *King report on corporate governance for South Africa*. Parktown, November.

King, M. (2009), *Corporate governance: Individuals emerge as chief providers of capital, Business Report*, 18 August, 14.

King, M.E., and Ajogwu, F. (2020), *Outcomes-based corporate governance: A modern approach to corporate governance*. Cape Town, SA: Juta Publishers.

PriceWaterhouseCoopers (PwC) (2018), *Integrated reporting: What's your value creation story?*. London.

Securities and Exchange Board of India (SEBI) (2017), *Submission of report of the Committee on corporate governance*, Press Release No. 60/2017.

Securities Commission Malaysia (2017), Malaysian code of corporate governance. Retrieved from https://www.sc.com.my/regulation/corporate-governance.

The Council of Experts Concerning the Corporate Governance Code (2015), *Japan's corporate governance code*.

The Council of Experts Concerning the Japanese Version of the Stewardship Code (2014), *Principles for responsible institutional investors "Japan's Stewardship Code"*. Retrieved from https://www.fsa.go.jp/en/refer/councils/stewardship/20140407.html.

3 Corporate governance and voluntary disclosure

A review of the literature

As discussed in the previous chapter, through a review of the corporate governance Codes that have aligned, or are in the process of aligning to the principles of integrated reporting, the link between corporate governance and disclosure concerns various areas of application. This chapter will be devoted to the major developments in the academic and professional literature on the link between corporate governance and voluntary disclosure. More specifically, it will analyse the most significant studies in four main lines of enquiry, namely, corporate governance and voluntary disclosure[1] (generally conceived), corporate governance and sustainability reporting, corporate governance and intellectual capital, and corporate governance and integrated reporting. The main observations will also be framed in light of the underlying theoretical perspectives (agency, stewardship, and resource dependence). As will be evident in the following sections, these four categories should not be perceived as rigid, but several interconnections and overlapping can be identified among them. Therefore, the main similarities and differences between the four areas emerging from this review will also be outlined.

Corporate governance and voluntary disclosure

In the academic literature, the association between corporate governance and voluntary disclosure has started to be investigated mainly during the 1990s by taking into consideration variables such as ownership structure (Craswell and Taylor, 1992; McKinnon and Dalimunthe, 1993; Raffournier, 1995), the presence of independent directors on the board (Forker, 1992; Malone et al., 1993), and the link to the inclusion of a discretionary set of information in annual reports, initially proxied by earnings forecast (Clarkson et al., 1994; Healy and Palepu, 2001; Bhat et al., 2006) and then expanded to more strategic, forward-looking, and non-financial information (O'Sullivan et al., 2008; Wang and Hussainey, 2013). Probably some of the key pioneer studies on this topic have been the ones by Jensen and Meckling (1976), Fama and Jensen (1983), Williamson (1985) and Jensen (1993).

Jensen and Meckling (1976) hold that internal governance mechanisms and practices are a fundamental tenet of agency theory in that they can ensure that managers act in the best interest of shareholders. This is particularly true in the presence of managerial ownership. In such situation, managers are in fact encouraged to improve the level and the quality of information, thus contributing to the creation of a transparent information environment. Always in the context of agency theory, Fama and Jensen (1983) further analyse the composition of the board in a situation where there is a strong separation between ownership and control, which is where managers do not hold shares of the company they work for. They observe that although the presence of internal managers in the board can be seen as a guarantee for effective decision-making since they have a "valuable specific knowledge about the organization's activity" (p. 314), it is with the appointment of outside directors that a company can actually improve the monitoring role of the board. Their 'independent' nature can ensure the interests of the organisation, and its shareholders, against the opportunistic behaviour of managers. On the contrary, a large size of the board can exacerbate agency costs in that it can become a source of communication and coordination problems, thus decreasing the monitoring role of the board towards managers (Jensen, 1993). Williamson (1985) departs from the view that the board of directors should give prominence to shareholders, but rather advances that it should act as an impartial body. He suggests that it "should be regarded primarily as a governance structure safeguard between the company and owners of equity capital and secondarily as a way by which to safeguard contractual relations between the company and its management" (p. 298).

These preliminary yet fundamental studies on the role of corporate governance in disclosure practices have then been expanded over the years to the examination of other countries. Following the Asian financial crisis that occurred during the 1990s, several scholars have examined if and to what extent corporate governance has yielded to a change in reporting practices. Ho and Wong (2001) investigated the role of independent non-executive directors, audit committee, dominant personalities (as a proxy of CEO duality) and family members on voluntary disclosure in a sample comprising all listed companies in Hong Kong. They found that, differently from previous studies, the presence of a large proportion of outside directors does not influence the disclosure of additional information, while the establishment of an audit committee able to internally monitor managerial behaviour does. The existence of a dominant personality embodied by the CEO being also the Chairman has not resulted to be particularly significant. This is mainly due to the fact that persons covering these roles tend to be shareholders of the company, thus a separation or not of the roles does not affect its level of disclosure. Differently from this, the presence of a family-controlled board is found to negatively influence corporate disclosure transparency. A higher proportion of family members on the board tend to lower the inclusion of voluntary information.

Always in the Asian setting, and particularly in Singapore, Eng and Mak (2003) focussed on the impact that ownership structure and board composition can have on corporate disclosure and particularly, on the voluntary disclosure of strategic, non-financial, and financial information in financial statements. In order to do so, three types of ownership structure are taken into consideration, namely, managerial ownership, conceived as the proportion of ordinary shares held by the CEO and executive directors, blockholder ownership, intended as the proportion of ordinary shares held by the majority of shareholders, and government ownership, which relates to the participation of the government in private companies. As for the composition of the board, it is measured by the percentage of external non-executive directors on the board. In terms of control variables, they control for the impact of growth opportunities, company size, debt, industry, the reputation of the auditors, the follow-up of the analysts, the trend of the share prices, and the propensity to disclose the company information. Based on a sample of 158 listed companies in Singapore in 1995, it resulted that the disclosure of voluntary information in financial statements increases when managerial ownership is reduced, while government ownership is significant. The total ownership of the block holder is not found to have an impact on this type of disclosure. As for board composition, the presence of a large proportion of external directors reduces voluntary disclosure. This is deemed to a 'substitute relationship' that exists between external directors and disclosure. Indeed, external directors can act as monitoring actors so as voluntary disclosure. With regard to the financial and economic characteristics of companies, the authors observed that larger and less indebted firms tend to issue more information on a voluntary basis. Gul and Leung (2004) examined the links between board structure, the presence of experienced external directors and the decision to issue voluntary information in annual reports. To do so, the examination has considered CEO duality, which relates to those situations when CEOs act jointly as board chair, and the percentage of experienced external directors on the board, which corresponds to those directors who sit on boards of other 'unrelated' companies. Analysis of observations of 385 Hong Kong listed companies in 1996 shows that the concentration of power by the CEO, represented by his/her duality, is associated with lower levels of voluntary corporate disclosure. In addition, not only the presence of Non-Executive Directors (NEDs) but their experience negatively influences the inclusion of voluntary information, in virtue of the higher degree of independence and competence that is attributed to the board. However, in the presence of a CEO duality, a large proportion of experienced NEDs can mitigate the negative association that exists with voluntary disclosure. Huafang and Jianguo (2007) examine the impact of the ownership structure and composition of the board of directors on the voluntary communications of listed companies in China. With the advent of a more aggressive competition by foreign companies, the government has in fact started to improve its corporate governance policies to prepare Chinese companies. In this respect, companies are required to include at least two independent directors on the board. In addition, these are called to comment on the adequacy of management actions in the company's annual reports. The sample is composed of 559 company observations from 2002. The results show that increased ownership of block holders and ownership of foreign stocks are associated with increased disclosure. However, managerial ownership, state ownership, and legal entity ownership are not related to disclosure. An increase in independent directors increases the disclosure of corporate information, and the duality of the CEO is associated with less disclosure. The document also notes that larger companies had greater disclosure, while companies with growth opportunities are reluctant to disclose information voluntarily. In summary, it turns out that greater ownership of block owners and significant foreign equity ownership are associated with greater voluntary disclosure. Managerial ownership, state ownership, and legal entity are not related to disclosure. An increase in the number of outsider directors improves voluntary disclosure and the duality of the CEO reduces disclosure. In replicating the study by Ho and Wong in the Malaysian context, Akhtaruddin et al. (2009) indicated that board size, independent non-executive directors and the amount of outside ownership are positively and significantly associated with voluntary disclosure, while family control negatively influences it. Differently from Ho and Wong, they observe that internal monitoring through audit committee members on the board does not affect this type of disclosure.

Moving to the European setting, and specifically to the Italian one which is characterised by a control function conducted by companies' owners and in general by a concentration of ownership as well as a perceived lack of independence of outside directors and a weak protection of small investors, Patelli and Prencipe (2007) examine the association between the existence of independent directors on the board and voluntary disclosure in 175 non-financial Italian companies characterised by the presence of dominant shareholders. This is because dominant shareholders are expected to mitigate agency-related problems. They observe that a positive relationship exists, i.e. internal control provided by independent directors tend to co-exist with external control provided by voluntary disclosure. Thus, contrary to Eng and Mak (2003) no substitution effect emerges. These results could also be amenable to the stricter definition of independent directors that the authors have followed, i.e. the one that excludes interlocking directorates and directors that sit on the same board for a long period. Allegrini and Greco (2013) investigated the relationship between corporate governance mechanisms, in terms of both structure and functioning, and voluntary disclosure. In analysing a sample of 177 Italian non-financial and listed companies in 2007, they found that voluntary disclosure in annual reports is influenced by larger boards that meet more frequently, but their composition as well as the presence of committees and lead independent directors do not impact it. The frequency of audit committees' meetings is also a factor which relates to additional discretionary disclosure. CEO duality is negatively, though poorly, associated with it. In general, this suggests that it becomes fundamental for companies to combine internal and external controls. Donnelly and Mulcahy (2008) investigated the role of board composition (proportion of non-executive directors), CEO duality, concentration of outside/managerial ownership on the voluntary disclosure of Irish companies. Ireland represents a unique case study in that it is influenced by both the UK and the US. Its legal and institutional environments are similar to those of the UK, but the business is permeated by the US culture through investments in Irish companies. The investigation has centred on 51 listed companies as of June 2002. Findings support the view that the greater the number of non-executive directors sitting on the board is, the greater is the tendency of companies to report information other than the mandated one. Differently from other studies, no evidence is found for the interrelationship with CEO duality and ownership concentration (both internal and external). In focussing on ownership concentration, Makhija and Patton (2004) examined the Czech context in a year of change, 1993. Until 1993 the ownership structure of Czech companies was largely external, and their annual financial report was voluntary in nature. The newly privatised companies hence represent an ideal setting where to test this relationship. Results from a sample of 43 non-financial firms illustrate that ownership and especially, investment fund ownership is a fundamental component influencing voluntary disclosure only when the concentration is low. In Spain, Arcay and Vazquez (2005) observed that ownership structure, cross-listing (in foreign markets included) and the presence of independent directors have an influence on corporate disclosure, and firm size results to be a significant determinant but with no effect on the adoption of good corporate governance practices. Similarly, belonging to a regulated industry does not affect the provision of voluntary information.

Barako et al. (2006) examined voluntary disclosure in a developing country, Kenya, where the government has initiated over the past decade several reforms on the Nairobi Stock Exchange in order to incentivise domestic savings and attract foreign capital. To do so, they examine the role of non-executive directors, of an audit committee and board leadership in a sample of listed companies between 1992 and 2001. It is observed that the presence of an audit committee and of institutional and foreign ownership is associated with this corporate attitude, while non-executive directors are negatively associated and board leadership is not.

In Australia Lim et al. (2007) concur with those previous studies that have found that the presence of an independent board positively influences voluntary disclosure, even though with a caveat. From the examination conducted on 181 companies, they observe that the association of board composition differs on the nature of information released. In particular, the presence of outside directors impacts on the choice of firms to include forward-looking and strategic information on their annual reports. No evidence is found on non-financial and historical financial set of information.

From the analysis conducted (summarised by Table 3.1), it is possible to note that it is difficult to identify a set of corporate governance internal variables able to generally explain the linkages with voluntary disclosure by companies. The presence of outside directors is probably the most adopted one, even though it has been demonstrated that its influence can sometimes diminish in situations where a substitution effect exists. As for ownership structure, this can be dependent from the economic, and legal context it is analysed. No homogeneous view

Table 3.1 Summary of main studies that have investigated the relationship between corporate governance and voluntary disclosure (focus on outside/inside directors)

Authors	Theoretical framework	Influence of outside directors on voluntary disclosure	Influence of inside directors on voluntary disclosure
Ho and Wong (2001)	Agency	No influence	–
Eng and Mak (2003)	Agency	Negative (substitution effect)	–
Gul and Leung (2004)	Agency	Negative (by experienced NEDs)	–
Huafang and Jianguo (2007)	Agency	Positive	–
Akhtaruddin et al. (2009)	Agency	Positive	–
Allegrini and Greco (2013)	Agency	Positive (by both internal – auditing committee – and external control)	–
Patelli and Prencipe (2007)	Agency	Positive (stricter definition of independent directors)	–
Donnelly and Mulcahy (2008)	Agency	Positive	–
Makhija and Patton (2004)	Agency	–	–
Arcay and Vazquez (2005)	Agency	Positive	–
Barako et al. (2006)	Agency	Negative	–
Lim et al. (2007)	Agency	Positive (for forward-looking and strategic information)	–

Source: Author's elaboration.

is achieved not even with reference to CEO duality. Interestingly to note, agency theory is the underlying one for all the papers here investigated. This further reinforces the assumption, already mentioned in Chapter 1, that agency theory tends to privilege the presence of non-executives, independent directors in order for the board to exert its control function on managers.

Corporate governance and sustainability reporting

The relationship between corporate governance and corporate social responsibility has been a widely debated one in the literature. Scholars and professionals have been interested in studying this possible association in different countries and sectors. This growing attention can be amenable to the occurrence of several corporate scandals, such as Enron and WorldCom that have heavily impacted on the international financial system. As a consequence, the interest by many (shareholders and stakeholders in general) has been directed to the way companies are governed. As anticipated in Chapter 1, corporate disclosure has been subject to an evolution that goes hand-in-hand with corporate governance. The culture that permeates from the board to the whole organisation impacts on the decision to report on a wider set of discretionary information that go beyond the mandated one. In turn, the reporting process affects the way the board of directors think and act. Hence, it is not surprising that the debate has shifted towards the relevance of non-financial factors, Environmental, Social and Governance (ESG) and intangibles aspects, and to long-term value creation, both for the boardroom and for corporate reporting (Ceres, 2015, 2017, 2018a, 2018b, 2019; FCLT Global, 2019; WBCSD, 2020).

This shift has also nurtured the academic debate, even though mainly starting from mid of the 2000s. Money and Schepers in 2007 noted that "there is little existing knowledge from a corporate perspective as to the extent of alignment between corporate governance and CSR" (p. 5). Some previous studies have used proxies, such as the country of origin (Laan Smith et al., 2005), later ones a limited number of corporate governance variables (Haniffa and Cooke, 2005; Faisal et al., 2012). Others have investigated the impact of wide range of variables on the environmental performance on companies, but not on their reporting practices (Wang and Coffey, 1992; Webb, 2004; Bear et al., 2010; De Villiers et al., 2011; Shaukat et al., 2016; Cuadrado-Ballesteros et al., 2017). Following these pioneer studies, Prado-Lorenzo et al. (2009) in the Spanish context represented by 99 non-financial listed companies observed that social disclosure can largely be explained by the pressure exerted by stakeholders as well as dispersed ownership structure. This is further reinforced by the presence of external directors on the board.

Michelon and Parbonetti (2012) examined the relationship between board composition, leadership, and structure and the disclosure of sustainability-related information in a comparative exercise between Europe and the US. Similarly to previous studies, they depart from the premises that a good corporate governance can represent a vehicle towards a better communication with stakeholders. It is in fact the board that takes decisions and enacts disclosure policies. They demonstrate that the traditional difference between insiders and independent directors is not sufficient to understand this relationship. The specific characteristics of each director then become fundamental. The sample is constituted by 57 Dow Jones Sustainability Index (DJSI) companies. From a methodological viewpoint, the disclosure index takes into consideration the contents not only on the annual reports, but also on other types of independent reports, such as social, environmental, and sustainability reports. Sustainability information is classified into four groups: strategic, financial, environmental, and social information. It is found that the composition of the board of directors, measured as the percentage of influential members of the community, positively affects sustainability, the environment, and strategic disclosure, and positively affects the choice to disclose information in independent reports. More specifically, it is not the large proportion of independent directors that influences the quantity and quality of sustainability information, rather their background. A positive association is generally found between the so-called community influential and sustainability disclosure – in separate reports – but also with two of the sub-categories of information that make up the total disclosure index, environmental, and strategic information. This is amenable to their ability to affect reporting media. A weak evidence is found for the relationship between the presence of a committee or CSR director and the disclosure of social information. In the US context Mallin et al. (2013) examined the impact of the corporate governance model on social and environmental disclosure. They centre the investigation on the top 100 US Best corporate citizens in the period 2005–2007 and examine both the quality and the quantity of social and environmental information in order to understand whether the disclosure can be seen as a real commitment by the board towards stakeholders or as a signal or a legitimacy tool. They found that a strong monitoring function exercised by the board increases this type of disclosure In the post- Sarbanes–Oxley Act (SOX) US context, Zhang et al. (2013) demonstrate that two are the key components of a board to adopt CSR disclosure, independence, and diversity in terms of presence of women.

The work by Khan et al. (2013) has probably been one of the first one on the investigation between the effect that the board of directors can have on corporate social responsibility disclosure, especially in an emerging market, i.e. in the annual reports of Bangladesh companies.

To put it differently, they aim to understand whether corporate governance can be seen as a determinant for ensuring, if not improving, corporate legitimacy. This is of particular interest because also Bangladesh has adopted a Western-style model of corporate governance which encourages directors' independence, the separation between the CEO and the Chairman as well as the establishment of an audit committee. To do so, variables such as ownership structure (managerial, public, foreign), the independence of the board of directors, the duality of the CEO and the presence of the audit committee have been taken into consideration. The period covered four years from 2005 to 2009. They observe that although there is a negative association with managerial ownership, this turns into a positive association and significant for export-oriented companies. This is probable due to the pressure exerted by stakeholders to rely on a broader set of information in their decision-making processes. Also public ownership, foreign ownership, independence of the board of directors and the presence of the audit committee have positive effects on the CSR disclosure. On the contrary, CEO duality does not have any effect. Lone et al. (2016) in examining this possible association in the annual and sustainability reports of Pakistani companies, after the introduction of the CSR voluntary guidelines by the Securities and Exchange Commission of the country aimed at encouraging companies to disclosure this type of information, observe that board independence, diversity (in terms of gender) and size affect this decision.

On the risk side, Peters and Romi (2014) examine the corporate governance characteristics associated with the voluntary disclosure of greenhouse gases by US companies in the period from 2002 to 2006. In particular, they focus on the existence of an environmental and an audit committee as accompanied by the presence of a Chief Sustainability Officer (CSO) considered as an executive-support position, whose experience is examined. According to the authors, the expertise of a CSO can be distinguished between 'reactive', when he/she has public relations expertise and 'proactive' when the expertise relies on environmental and social basis. They observe that the presence of an environmental committee is a determinant for the decision to release GHG disclosure; however, once the decision is taken, its role diminishes disclosure transparency. As for the presence of a CSO, it appears to be key in terms of transparency, but not for the decision to report this set of information. More generally, the size and the activity of the environmental committee and its overlap with an audit committee positively influence GHG disclosure.

In Europe, and specifically in Spain, Fuente et al. (2017) examine the disclosure of CSR-related information according to the Global Reporting Initiative (GRI) standards in a sample of 98 non-financial listed Spanish companies over a six-year period. They point out that the presence of independent and proprietor directors is key in encouraging companies in implementing this disclosure practices. Furthermore, in terms of CSR standards adopted, the existence of a CSR committee is correlated to the GRI ones. Ramon-Llorens et al. (2019) further refine the analysis of board characteristics and point out that CEO power is key in encouraging outside directors, and specifically business experts and support specialists in adopting CSR reporting. However, it is not sufficient to compensate the negative effect of directors with political ties. In the UK, Jizi (2017) investigates this linkage in a sample of FTSE 350 firms for a five-year period. It is noted that board independence as well as women presence are a determinant for CSR reporting.

In Australia, Rao and Tilt (2016) investigate the extent to which board composition, and in particular its diversity, impacts on CSR reporting by taking into consideration five corporate governance variables, namely, independence, tenure, gender, multiple directorships, and overall diversity measure. The sample is composed of 150 listed companies over a three-year period. It is observed that all the variables positively affect this type of reporting disclosure, with the exception of independent directors.

In enlarging the sample to a cross-national one, Ibrahim and Angelidis already in 1995 outlined that differences between inside and outside directors exist vis-à-vis the so-called corporate social responsibility orientation and financial performance. Outside directors result to be more inclined to consider ESG factors, rather than traditional economic and financial ones. This has been confirmed also in organisations operating in the service industry (Ibrahim et al., 2003) and more recently, by the meta-analysis of the literature conducted by Guerrero-Villegas et al. (2018), even though the latter further notice that this linkage can be influenced by the institutional setting – level of commitment to sustainable goals.

Also in the case of CSR disclosure, no convergence is achieved on the features that can encourage companies to disclose sustainability-related information (Table 3.2). Interestingly to note, the independence of the board has emerged as being a variable that is in most of the cases positively associated with it under different theoretical assumptions.

Table 3.2 Summary of main studies that have investigated the relationship between corporate governance and CSR disclosure (focus on outside/inside directors)

Authors	Theoretical framework	Influence of outside directors on voluntary disclosure	Influence of inside directors on voluntary disclosure
Prado-Lorenzo et al. (2009)	Stakeholder	Positive	–
Michelon and Parbonetti (2012)	Resource-dependence	Positive (community influential)	–
Mallin et al. (2013)	Agency	Positive	–
Zhang et al. (2013)	Legitimacy	Positive	–
Khan et al. (2013)	Legitimacy	Positive	–
Lone et al. (2016)	Agency	Positive	–
Peters and Romi (2014)	Agency	–	–
Fuente et al. (2017)	Legitimacy and stakeholder	Positive	–
Jizi (2017)	Agency	Positive	–
Rao and Tilt (2016)	Agency	Unclear	–
Ibrahim and Angelidis (1995)	–	Positive	–
Ibrahim et al. (2003)	–	Positive	–
Guerrero-Villegas et al. (2018)	–	Positive	–

Source: Author's elaboration.

Corporate governance and intellectual capital reporting

The disclosure of value creation and intellectual capital has received increasing attention from companies around the world. This is mainly due to the new economy, which is a knowledge-based economy where value creation becomes one of the crucial issues in the world and tends to be based on intangible rather than tangible assets. Intellectual capital is increasingly important in creating and maintaining competitive advantage and stakeholder value. However, financial statements do not always reflect such a wide range of sources of value creation, resulting in information asymmetries between businesses and users. This creates inefficiencies in the process of allocating resources in capital markets. As a result, markets increasingly require more disclosure of non-financial information and investment indicators of intangible assets.

In the European context, Cerbioni and Parbonetti first (2007) and Li et al. (2008) after, found that some corporate governance variables can influence the disclosure (in terms of quantity and/or quality) of intellectual capital. In a sample of 54 European biotechnology firms listed on the stock market of a European country, Cerbioni and Parbonetti (2007) have analysed the impact of a company's board size, composition (in terms of proportion of independent outside directors), CEO duality, and board structure on the type and amount of intellectual capital an organisation discloses. The examination is conducted on their Operating Financial Reviews in the period from 2002 to 2014 (included). Evidence demonstrates that board structure, CEO duality, and size are negatively correlated with disclosure, while the proportion of independent directors is positively associated. However, in terms of quality of the disclosure, it is found that the presence of independent directors affects only information on internal capital. This is not the case for the disclosure of forward-looking information and bad news. Li et al. (2008) have examined if and how the corporate governance characteristics of 100 UK firms listed on the London Stock Exchange and belonging to seven intellectual capital-intensive industries can influence intellectual capital disclosure in annual reports. The time period is for financial year-ends between March 2004 and February 2005. Taking into consideration five characteristics (board composition in terms of proportion of independent non-executive directors, role duality, ownership structure/share concentration, audit committee size, and frequency of meetings), they observe that role duality is not found to influence intellectual capital disclosure and that share ownership concentration is negatively associated with it, meaning that in the presence of dominant shareholders there is less pressure for the reporting of this type of information. The other three variables are found to be significantly and positively associated. As for the influence that corporate governance mechanisms have on the disclosure on the three sub-categories of intellectual capital, human, structural/organisational, and relational, it results that the presence of independent non-executive directors results in the disclosure of more information related to human, structural, and relational capitals, while the presence of block shareholders appears to lead to more disclosure on relational capital.

In Italy, Baldini and Liberatore (2016) study the association between some corporate governance internal mechanisms and the level of intellectual capital disclosure in general and of its main components, investigating the annual reports of 172 listed companies on 31 December 2010. Their findings indicated that only board size and board independence have a significant positive effect. In Portugal, Rodrigues et al. (2017) explore the influence of boards of directors on the voluntary disclosure of information concerning intellectual capital of 15 listed companies over a period of five years during the Portuguese financial crisis. In analysing IC disclosure in annual, sustainability, and integrated reports, they find that it remains constant even during this particular time. More specifically, it increases with dual corporate governance models and with a larger board size up to a maximum point (thus confirming a quadratic relationship) but is reduced by CEO duality and by a higher proportion of independent directors on boards. The presence of women on the board is not found to be statistically significant. In Spain, Tejedo-Romero et al. (2017) analyse the sustainability reports of the 25 listed companies on IBEX 35 share market index over a period of five years (2007–2011). More specifically, they examine the effect of the board size, board activity, board independence and ownership concentration on Intellectual Capital Disclosure (ICD). Their results find that a higher presence of women in the board is positively associated with ICD. On the contrary, board activity and the presence of external independent directors are negatively associated. Board size and ownership concentration are not found to be significant.

In developing countries, Abeysekera (2010) explores the influence of board size on six types of ICD, conducting this analysis on the annual reports of the top 26 Kenyan listed companies in 2002 and 2003. It is demonstrated that the firms with larger boards tend to disclose more information on strategic human capital and tactical internal (organisational) capital, while no influence is shown between board size and external (relationship) capital. The presence of independent directors results to be significant on ICD and in particular on tactical human capital when they sit on committees other the audit one. The positive impact of board size on the ICD disclosure is also confirmed in the Mexican context by the study of Hidalgo et al. (2011), even though in quadratic terms (larger boards yield benefits up to a point). In contrast, they find a negative association with shareholding by institutional investors as well as by the company. No association is indicated with board independence and the size of the audit committee. In Malaysia,

Taliyang and Jusop (2011) carried out an investigation to study the extent of disclosure of intellectual capital and the relationship between this disclosure and corporate governance variables in a sample of 150 companies listed in Bursa in Malaysia, covering five sectors (IT, consumer product, industrial product, services, and finance). Malaysian companies should in fact disclose intellectual capital in their annual reports on a voluntary basis. The independent variables tested in this study include various forms of corporate governance structure, namely, the composition of the board of directors, CEO duality, size of the audit committee and frequency of meetings of the audit committee. It is found that the majority of the companies examined include intellectual capital information in their annual reports (mainly in financial statements and in the notes to the financial statements, director's report, the corporate governance statement, and other operational reports). This is particularly the case of knowledge-intensive sectors, such as the financial and the IT ones. As for the four corporate governance variables tested, only the frequency of meetings of the audit committee has demonstrated a significant positive relationship in influencing the level of disclosure of intellectual capital in Malaysia, while there is no significant relationship between the composition of the board of directors, dual role of the CEO, and the size of the audit committee. It shows that the more regular meetings the company held, the more it encourages directors to disclose voluntary information in their annual report. In the same country, Haji and Ghazali (2013) explored the extent and quality of ICD by top listed companies on Bursa Malaysia for the period 2008–2010. The results suggest that all the corporate governance variables taken into consideration, namely, board size, independent directors, board effectiveness, and position of the Chairman (except family members on the board), do explain the extent and quality of ICD. Director ownership is not related to both the extent and quality of ICDs. Government ownership is only marginally significant.

Finally, in an emerging country such as Bangladesh, the research by Muttakin et al. (2015) confirms that family ownership negatively affects ICD as well as family duality. This strong influence by the family renders the presence of CEO duality neutral. Foreign ownership, board independence, and the presence of an audit committee positively influences the disclosure of this type of information.

Similarly to the review conducted on linkages between corporate governance, voluntary, and CSR disclosure, also in the case of intellectual capital, there is no consensus on what are the key determinants

(Table 3.3). The proportion of outside directors has shown to be the most investigated variable and in the majority of cases is found to be positively associated with this type of reporting practice. However, the same cannot be said with reference to the quality of information disclosed. The presence of women in the boardroom has also resulted to be one of the characteristics that positively influences the reporting of intangibles-related information. From a theoretical perspective, it is possible to observe that the positive association between boards' independence and intellectual capital reporting is mostly explained in light of agency theory. Some studies have outlined that it can become negative if a resource-based theory is adopted (either in conjunction or not).

Table 3.3 Summary of main studies that have investigated the relationship between corporate governance and intellectual capital disclosure (focus on outside/inside directors)

Authors	Theoretical framework	Influence of outside directors on voluntary disclosure	Influence of inside directors on voluntary disclosure
Cerbioni and Parbonetti (2007)	Agency	Positive	–
Li et al. (2008)	Agency	Positive	–
Baldini and Liberatore (2016)	Agency	Positive	–
Rodrigues et al. (2017)	Agency and resource-based	Negative	–
Tejedo-Romero et al. (2017)	Resource-dependence	Negative	–
Abeysekera (2010)	Resource-dependence	Positive	–
Hidalgo et al. (2011)	Agency	No association	–
Taliyang and Jusop (2011)	Agency	No association	–
Haji and Ghazali (2013)	Agency	Positive	–
Muttakin et al. (2015)	Agency	Positive	

Source: Author's elaboration.

Corporate governance and integrated reporting

Despite the inherent link that exists between corporate governance and integrated reporting, to date only a peripheral number of studies have investigated which are the board characteristics that can act as determinants of the voluntary adoption and, or the quality, of integrated reporting (Eccles and Serafeim, 2011; Mähönen, 2020).

As for the former, Frias-Aceituno et al. (2013) analysed a sample of 568 companies from 15 countries, for the period 2008–2010. They argue that some board characteristics (board size, board diversity, the composition of the board) in reducing the information asymmetries between managers and stakeholders can impact on the decision to disclose integrated information. The results of this study show that only board size and board gender diversity have a role in the decision of companies to publish the integrated reporting. The same results are confirmed by a later study by Fiori et al. (2016), which examines only the firms participating in the IIRC Pilot Programme launched by the IIRC in 2011 with the aim to encourage the development of integrated reporting and create a common framework. Two samples of European companies are taken into consideration, a sample of 35 companies that joined the pilot programme in 2011 which has been confronted with a sample of 137 companies that did not join. The governance variables that have been used are the size of the board, frequency of meetings, the presence of non-executive directors, of a block holder and of women. The size of the board and the presence of women are found to be two main determinants in the decision of companies to join the pilot programme. The frequency of meetings is positive but not statistically significant. As for the role of independent directors and the presence of a block holder, they are associated with a lower probability of joining the programme. Also Alfiero et al. (2017) in focussing on the European setting observed that in a sample of 1,047 companies from 18 countries adopting this reporting tool in 2015 board size, the presence of women and an average age of 55 years of board members are positively associated. Girella et al. (2019) extend the latter works analysing the companies considered <IR> Reporters by the IIRC according to the <IR> Examples Databases. However, they found that only the size of the board is a determinant, while the presence of women and of independent directors is not. Garcia-Sanchez et al. (2019) have investigated this possible association in a munificence context, which is when an industry witnesses an abundance of resources. By means of a principal component analysis of board characteristics that synthetises its effectiveness, namely, independence, gender diversity, experience, expertise, and the probability of referring an external consultants applied to an international sample composed of 956 firms belonging to different industries and 27 countries through a longitudinal period (2006–2014), they observed that the strength of the board can diminish the discretionary role of managers in disclosing less voluntary information. Suttipun and Bomlai (2019) carried out a study to investigate the extent and level of integrated reporting in the annual reports of Thai stock exchange listed companies between 2012 and 2015 through a random sample of 150 companies. The results did not find a significant correlation between the level of integrated reporting and family-owned companies, government-owned companies, the percentage of independent members of the boards of directors and the duality of CEOs. This can be related to the lack of regulations that require reporting in developing countries, so that there is no pressure on companies to carry out voluntary relationships, including integrated reporting.

In the impression management strategies literature, Melloni et al. (2016) and Busco et al (2019), adopting a manual content analysis and a statistical investigation of all the reports identified as emerging practices in the IIRC Examples Database and in the Stoxx Europe 600 Index for the period 2002–2015, document, respectively, the drivers of the tone of business models and the different levels of information integration. In the first study, the authors find that bigger boards influence the positive tone of business model disclosure, thus decreasing the reports' transparency and increasing the possible manipulation of information by management. The presence of independent members in the auditing committees is not significantly associated. The results of the second study confirm that only board size influences the levels of integration, but the frequencies of meetings and the independence of the boards do not. Stacchezzini et al. (2016) concur with the results of these works in advancing that impression management strategies can drive the adoption of integrated reporting. On the contrary, Lai et al. (2016) maintained that the companies joining the IIRC Pilot Programme have not decided to do so for legitimacy reasons.

Moving to the quality of the reports, Barth et al. (2017) in the South African setting examine the capital markets and real effects associated with the quality of integrated reporting. By using data from the 100 top listed companies on the Johannesburg Stock Exchange ranked as leading practices by E&Y, they observe that quality is associated with liquidity and expected future cash flows, but not with cost of capital. Wang et al. (2020), integrating economic-based and sociopolitical theories, investigate the relationship with traditional and sustainability-oriented corporate governance mechanisms and the credibility of integrated reporting in the South African context. Their results show that traditional corporate governance measures such as the quality of the board and the audit committee (intended as a composite score of independence, diligence, size, and expertise of both) have a lower impact than the presence of a high-quality sustainability committee and non-financial performance measures in executive compensation. In an international sample of 134 firms selected from the Leading Practices and the <IR> Reporters section of the IIRC Examples Database, Vitolla et al. (2020) found that size, independence, gender diversity, and activity of the board determine a high quality of the documents, while the presence of a CSR committee does not. In focussing on the quality of a particular but fundamental element of integrated report, materiality, Fasan and Mio (2017) documented that the board size and gender diversity are negatively associated with it, while positively with board independence, activity, and the presence of civil law. Gerwanski et al. (2019), in replicating the study of Fasan and Mio by taking into consideration the only variable gender diversity (as for corporate governance) in an international sample of companies for a later period (2013–2016), found that gender diversity is positively associated with the quality of materiality. In a similar vein, Kılıç and Kuzey (2018) examined if corporate governance internal mechanisms can influence the disclosure of another fundamental concept of integrated report, forward-looking information. In a sample of 55 non-financial firms extracted from the <IR> Examples Database for the year 2014, they found that only gender diversity is significantly and positively associated with the total, quantitative, and qualitative forward-looking disclosure. Board size and board composition are not. This is consistent with those previous studies according to which the presence of different backgrounds and ethnicities has become a relevant tenet of corporate governance. As for the potential relationship between corporate governance and integrated reporting quality, measured as the assurance of these reports, Kılıç et al. (2019) found that less effective boards tend to yield companies to privilege this practice.

When it comes to an innovative accountability tool, as integrated reporting can be, corporate governance attributes result to impact in a different ways on its adoption on the basis of the underlying theoretical framework. If the presence of a diverse board (existence of women) is able to explain in the majority of cases of implementation and also of quality, the same cannot be said with reference to board independence (Table 3.4) (Velte and Gerwanski, 2020).

Table 3.4 Summary of main studies that have investigated the relationship between corporate governance and integrated reporting (focus on outside/inside directors)

Authors	Theoretical framework	Influence of outside directors on voluntary disclosure	Influence of inside directors on voluntary disclosure
Frias-Aceituno et al. (2013)	Agency	No association	–
Fiori et al. (2016)	Agency	Low association	–
Alfiero et al. (2017)	Agency	–	–
Girella et al. (2019)	Agency Signalling Cost of Capital Political Cost Proprietary Costs Institutional Stakeholder	No association	–
Garcia-Sanchez et al. (2019)	Resource-dependence	Positive	–
Suttipun and Bomlai (2019)	Legitimacy and agency	No association	–
Lai et al. (2016)	Legitimacy	–	–
Melloni et al. (2016)	Agency	No association	–
Busco et al (2019)	Stakeholder	No association	–

Source: Author's elaboration.

Conclusion

In this chapter the main developments in the academic and professional literature on the link between corporate governance and voluntary disclosure have been discussed. More specifically, an investigation of the most significant studies in four key lines of enquiry, namely, corporate governance and voluntary disclosure, corporate governance and sustainability reporting, corporate governance and intellectual capital, and corporate governance and integrated reporting have been conducted. It is possible to note that no homogeneous views exist on which are the corporate governance mechanisms that are considered the most influential in the implementation of voluntary forms of corporate reporting.

Furthermore, in regard to the relationship between corporate governance and integrated reporting, the review of the literature conducted reveals that the following two are the topics that still appear in need for a more profound and solid understanding:

The nexus between the financial state of companies first adopting integrated reporting and their corporate governance, and in particular the professional backgrounds of their boards, which is useful to shed light also on the "impression management assumption" put forward in the literature reviewed that resumes a linkage between the adoption of this form of accountability and the difficult financial situation of companies.

The nexus between the decision to uptake integrated reporting by a company and the composition of its board and the associated professional background and expertise (Gray and Nowland, 2013).

The above two issues seem to be quite open in the literature and subject to different theoretical interpretations and empirical analyses. Therefore, they will be the focal points of the analysis that will be carried out in the next chapter.

Note

1 Although the author is aware that several studies have also been developed on (a) the linkages between the disclosure of corporate governance practices and the extent of corporate voluntary disclosure and (b) corporate governance and the quality of voluntary disclosure, these topics are outside the scope of this book.

Bibliography

Abeysekera, I. (2010), The influence of board size on intellectual capital disclosure by Kenyan listed firms. *Journal of Intellectual Capital*, *11*(4), 504–518.

Akhtaruddin, M., Hossain, M. A., Hossain, M., and Yao, L. (2009), Corporate governance and voluntary disclosure in corporate annual reports of Malaysian listed firms. *Journal of Applied Management Accounting Research*, *7*(1), 1–20.

Alfiero, S., Cane, M., Doronzo, R., and Esposito, A. (2017), Board configuration and IR adoption. Empirical evidence from European companies. *Corporate Ownership & Control*, *15*(1–2), 444–458.

Allegrini, M., and Greco, G. (2013), Corporate boards, audit committees and voluntary disclosure: Evidence from Italian listed companies. *Journal of Management & Governance*, *17*(1), 187–216.

Arcay, M. R. B., and Vázquez, M. F. M. (2005), Corporate characteristics, governance rules and the extent of voluntary disclosure in Spain. *Advances in Accounting, 21,* 299–331.

Baldini, M. A., and Liberatore, G. (2016), Corporate governance and intellectual capital disclosure. An empirical analysis of the Italian listed companies. *Corporate Ownership and Control, 13*(2), 187–201.

Barako, D. G., Hancock, P., and Izan, H. Y. (2006), Factors influencing voluntary corporate disclosure by Kenyan companies. *Corporate Governance: An International Review, 14*(2), 107–125.

Barth, M. E., Cahan, S. F., Chen, L., and Venter, E. R. (2017), The economic consequences associated with integrated report quality: Capital market and real effects, *Accounting, Organizations and Society, 62,* 43–64.

Bear, S., Rahman, N., and Post, C. (2010), The impact of board diversity and gender composition on corporate social responsibility and firm reputation. *Journal of Business Ethics, 97*(2), 207–221.

Bhat, G., Hope, O. K., and Kang, T. (2006), Does corporate governance transparency affect the accuracy of analyst forecasts?, *Accounting & Finance, 46*(5), 715–732.

Busco, C., Malafronte, I., Pereira, J., and Starita, M. G. (2019), The determinants of companies' levels of integration: Does one size fit all?. *The British Accounting Review, 51*(3), 277–298.

Cerbioni, F., and Parbonetti, A. (2007), Exploring the effects of corporate governance on intellectual capital disclosure: An analysis of European biotechnology companies. *European Accounting Review, 16*(4), 791–826.

Ceres (2015), *View from the top: How corporate boards can engage on sustainability performance.* Retrieved from https://www.ceres.org/resources/reports/view-top-how-corporate-boards-engage-sustainability-performance. Accessed on 27 August 2020.

Ceres (2017), *Lead from the top: Building sustainability competence on corporate boards.* Retrieved from https://www.ceres.org/resources/reports/lead-from-the-top. Accessed on 27 August 2020.

Ceres (2018a), *Getting climate smart: A primer for corporate directors in a changing environment.* Retrieved from https://www.ceres.org/climatesmartboards. Accessed on 27 August 2020.

Ceres (2018b), *Systems rule: How board governance can drive sustainability performance.* Retrieved from https://www.ceres.org/systemsrule. Accessed on 27 August 2020.

Ceres (2019), *Running the risk: How corporate boards can oversee environmental, social and governance (ESG) issues.* Retrieved from https://www.ceres.org/resources/reports/running-risk-how-corporate-boards-can-oversee-environmental-social-and-governance. Accessed on 27 August 2020.

Clarkson, P. M., Kao, P. J., and Richardson, G. (1994), The inclusion of forecasts in the MDA Section of annual reports: A voluntary disclosure perspective. *Contemporary Accounting Research, 11,* 423–450.

Craswell, A. T., and Taylor, S. L. (1992), Discretionary disclosure of reserves by oil and gas companies: An economic analysis. *Journal of Business Finance & Accounting, 19*(2), 295–308.

Cuadrado-Ballesteros, B., Martínez-Ferrero, J., and García-Sánchez, I. M. (2017), Board structure to enhance social responsibility development: A qualitative comparative analysis of US companies. *Corporate Social Responsibility and Environmental Management, 24*(6), 524–542.

De Villiers, C., Naiker, V., and Van Staden, C. J. (2011), The effect of board characteristics on firm environmental performance. *Journal of Management, 37*(6), 1636–1663.

Donnelly, R., and Mulcahy, M. (2008), Board structure, ownership, and voluntary disclosure in Ireland. *Corporate Governance: An International Review, 16*(5), 416–429.

Eccles, R. G., and Serafeim, G. (2011), The role of the board in accelerating the adoption of integrated reporting, *Director Notes (The Conference Board),* (November).

Eng, L. L., and Mak, Y. T. (2003), Corporate governance and voluntary disclosure. *Journal of Accounting and Public Policy, 22*(4), 325–345.

Faisal, F., Tower, G., and Rusmin, R. (2012), Legitimising corporate sustainability reporting throughout the world. *Australasian Accounting, Business and Finance Journal, 6*(2), 19–34.

Fama, E. F., and Jensen, M. C. (1983), Separation of ownership and control. *The Journal of Law and Economics, 26*(2), 301–325.

Fasan, M., and Mio, C. (2017), Fostering stakeholder engagement: The role of materiality disclosure in integrated reporting. *Business Strategy and the Environment, 26*(3), 288–305.

FCLT Global (2019), *The long-term habits of a highly effective corporate board.* Retrieved from https://www.fcltglobal.org/resource/the-long-term-habits-of-a-highly-effective-corporate-board/. Accessed on 13 July 2020.

Fiori, G., di Donato, F., and Izzo, M.F. (2016), Exploring the effects of corporate governance on voluntary disclosure: An explanatory study on the adoption of integrated report, in *Performance Measurement and Management Control: Contemporary Issues (Studies in Managerial and Financial Accounting, Vol. 31)*, Emerald Group Publishing Limited, 83–108.

Forker, J. J. (1992), Corporate governance and disclosure quality. *Accounting and Business Research, 22*(86), 111–124.

Frias-Aceituno, J. V., Rodriguez-Ariza, L., and Garcia-Sanchez, I. M. (2013), The role of the board in the dissemination of integrated corporate social reporting. *Corporate Social Responsibility and Environmental Management, 20*(4), 219–233.

Fuente, J. A., García-Sanchez, I. M., and Lozano, M. B. (2017), The role of the board of directors in the adoption of GRI guidelines for the disclosure of CSR information. *Journal of Cleaner Production, 141*, 737–750.

García-Sánchez, I. M., Martínez-Ferrero, J., and Garcia-Benau, M. A. (2019), Integrated reporting: The mediating role of the board of directors and investor protection on managerial discretion in munificent environments. *Corporate Social Responsibility and Environmental Management, 26*(1), 29–45.

Gerwanski, J., Kordsachia, O., and Velte, P. (2019), Determinants of materiality disclosure quality in integrated reporting: Empirical evidence from an international setting. *Business Strategy and the Environment, 28*(5), 750–770.

Girella, L., Rossi, P., and Zambon, S. (2019), Exploring the firm and country determinants of the voluntary adoption of integrated reporting. *Business Strategy and the Environment, 28*(7), 1323–1340.

Gray, S., and Nowland, J. (2013), Is prior director experience valuable?, *Accounting & Finance, 53*(3), 643–666.

Guerrero-Villegas, J., Pérez-Calero, L., Hurtado-González, J. M., and Giráldez-Puig, P. (2018), Board attributes and corporate social responsibility disclosure: A meta-analysis. *Sustainability, 10*(12), 4808.

Gul, F. A., and Leung, S. (2004), Board leadership, outside directors' expertise and voluntary corporate disclosures. *Journal of Accounting and public Policy, 23*(5), 351–379.

Haji, A. A., and Ghazali, N. A. M. (2013), A longitudinal examination of intellectual capital disclosures and corporate governance attributes in Malaysia. *Asian Review of Accounting, 21*(1), 27–52.

Haniffa, R. M., and Cooke, T. E. (2005), The impact of culture and governance on corporate social reporting. *Journal of Accounting and Public Policy, 24*(5), 391–430.

Healy, P. M., and Palepu, K. G. (2001), Information asymmetry, corporate disclosure, and the capital markets: A review of the empirical disclosure literature. *Journal of Accounting and Economics, 31*(1–3), 405–440.

Hidalgo, R. L., García-Meca, E., and Martínez, I. (2011), Corporate governance and intellectual capital disclosure. *Journal of Business Ethics, 100*(3), 483–495.

Ho, S. S., and Wong, K. S. (2001), A study of the relationship between corporate governance structures and the extent of voluntary disclosure. *Journal of International Accounting, Auditing and Taxation, 10*(2), 139–156.

Huafang, X., and Jianguo, Y. (2007), Ownership structure, board composition and corporate voluntary disclosure. *Managerial Auditing Journal, 22*(6), 604–619.

Ibrahim, N. A., and Angelidis, J. P. (1995), The corporate social responsiveness orientation of board members: Are there differences between inside and outside directors?, *Journal of Business Ethics, 14*(5), 405–410.

Ibrahim, N. A., Howard, D. P., and Angelidis, J. P. (2003), Board members in the service industry: An empirical examination of the relationship between corporate social responsibility orientation and directorial type. *Journal of Business Ethics, 47*(4), 393–401.

Jensen, M. C. (1993), The modern industrial revolution, exit, and the failure of internal control systems. *The Journal of Finance, 48*(3), 831–880.

Jensen, M. C., and Meckling, W. H. (1976), Theory of the firm: Managerial behavior, agency costs and ownership structure. *Journal of Financial Economics, 3*(4), 305–360.

Jizi, M. (2017), The influence of board composition on sustainable development disclosure, *Business Strategy and the Environment, 26*(5), 640–655.

Khan, A., Muttakin, M. B., and Siddiqui, J. (2013), Corporate governance and corporate social responsibility disclosures: Evidence from an emerging economy. *Journal of Business Ethics, 114*(2), 207–223.

Kılıç, M., and Kuzey, C. (2018), Determinants of forward-looking disclosures in integrated reporting. *Managerial Auditing Journal, 33*(1), 115–144.

Kılıç, M., Uyar, A., & Kuzey, C. (2019), The impact of institutional ethics and accountability on voluntary assurance for integrated reporting. *Journal of Applied Accounting Research, 21*(1), 1–18.

Lai, A., Melloni, G., and Stacchezzini, R. (2016), Corporate sustainable development: Is 'integrated reporting' a legitimation strategy?. *Business Strategy and the Environment, 25*(3), 165–177.

Li, J., Pike, R., and Haniffa, R. (2008), Intellectual capital disclosure and corporate governance structure in UK firms. *Accounting and Business Research, 38*(2), 137–159.

Lim, S., Matolcsy, Z., and Chow, D. (2007), The association between board composition and different types of voluntary disclosure. *European Accounting Review, 16*(3), 555–583.

Lone, E. J., Ali, A., and Khan, I. (2016), Corporate governance and corporate social responsibility disclosure: Evidence from Pakistan. *Corporate Governance: The International Journal of Business in Society, 16*(5), 785–797.

Mähönen, J. (2020), Integrated reporting and sustainable corporate governance from European perspective. *Accounting, Economics, and Law: A Convivium, 10*(2), (ahead-of-print).

Makhija, A. K., and Patton, J. M. (2004), The impact of firm ownership structure on voluntary disclosure: Empirical evidence from Czech annual reports. *The Journal of Business, 77*(3), 457–491.

Mallin, C., Michelon, G., and Raggi, D. (2013), Monitoring intensity and stakeholders' orientation: How does governance affect social and environmental disclosure?. *Journal of Business Ethics, 114*(1), 29–43.

Malone, D., Fries, C., and Jones, T. (1993), An empirical investigation of the extent of corporate financial disclosure in the oil and gas industry. *Journal of Accounting, Auditing & Finance, 8*(3), 249–273.

McKinnon, J. L., and Dalimunthe, L. (1993), Voluntary disclosure of segment information by Australian diversified companies. *Accounting & Finance, 33*(1), 33–50.

Melloni, G., Stacchezzini, R., and Lai, A. (2016), The tone of business model disclosure: An impression management analysis of the integrated reports. *Journal of Management & Governance, 20*(2), 295–320.

Michelon, G., and Parbonetti, A. (2012), The effect of corporate governance on sustainability disclosure. *Journal of Management & Governance, 16*(3), 477–509.

Money, K., and Schepers, H. (2007), Are CSR and corporate governance converging?: A view from boardroom directors and company secretaries in FTSE100 companies in the UK. *Journal of General Management, 33*(2), 1–11.

Muttakin, M. B., Khan, A., and Belal, A. R. (2015), Intellectual capital disclosures and corporate governance: An empirical examination. *Advances in Accounting, 31*(2), 219–227.

O'Sullivan, M., Percy, M., and Stewart, J. (2008), Australian evidence on corporate governance attributes and their association with forward-looking information in the annual report. *Journal of Management & Governance, 12*(1), 5–35.

Patelli, L., and Prencipe, A. (2007), The relationship between voluntary disclosure and independent directors in the presence of a dominant shareholder. *European Accounting Review, 16*(1), 5–33.

Peters, G. F., and Romi, A. M. (2014), Does the voluntary adoption of corporate governance mechanisms improve environmental risk disclosures? Evidence from greenhouse gas emission accounting. *Journal of Business Ethics, 125*(4), 637–666.

Prado-Lorenzo, J. M., Gallego-Alvarez, I., and Garcia-Sanchez, I. M. (2009), Stakeholder engagement and corporate social responsibility reporting: The ownership structure effect. *Corporate Social Responsibility and Environmental Management, 16*(2), 94–107.

Raffournier, B. (1995), The determinants of voluntary financial disclosure by Swiss listed companies. *European Accounting Review, 4*(2), 261–280.

Ramón-Llorens, M. C., García-Meca, E., and Pucheta-Martínez, M. C. (2019), The role of human and social board capital in driving CSR reporting. *Long Range Planning, 52*(6), 101846.

Rao, K., and Tilt, C. (2016), Board diversity and CSR reporting: An Australian study. *Meditari Accountancy Research, 24*(2), 182–210.

Rodrigues, L. L., Tejedo-Romero, F., and Craig, R. (2017), Corporate governance and intellectual capital reporting in a period of financial crisis: Evidence from Portugal. *International Journal of Disclosure and Governance, 14*(1), 1–29.

Shaukat, A., Qiu, Y., and Trojanowski, G. (2016), Board attributes, corporate social responsibility strategy, and corporate environmental and social performance. *Journal of Business Ethics, 135*(3), 569–585.

Stacchezzini, R., Melloni, G., and Lai, A. (2016), Sustainability management and reporting: The role of integrated reporting for communicating corporate sustainability management. *Journal of Cleaner Production, 136*, 102–110.

Suttipun, M., and Bomlai, A. (2019), The relationship between corporate governance and integrated reporting: Thai evidence. *International Journal of Business & Society, 20*(1), 348–364.

Taliyang, S. M., and Jusop, M. (2011), Intellectual capital disclosure and corporate governance structure: Evidence in Malaysia. *International Journal of Business and Management, 6*(12), 109.

Tejedo-Romero, F., Rodrigues, L. L., and Craig, R. (2017), Women directors and disclosure of intellectual capital information. *European Research on Management and Business Economics, 23*(3), 123–131.

Van der Laan Smith, J., Adhikari, A., and Tondkar, R. H. (2005), Exploring differences in social disclosures internationally: A stakeholder perspective. *Journal of Accounting and Public Policy, 24*(2), 123–151.

Velte, P., and Gerwanski, J. (2020), The impact of governance on integrated reporting, in *The Routledge handbook of integrated reporting*, (Eds. De Villiers, C., Hsiao, P. K., Maroun, W.) (2020), London: Routledge.

Vitolla, F., Raimo, N., and Rubino, M. (2020), Board characteristics and integrated reporting quality: an agency theory perspective. *Corporate Social Responsibility and Environmental Management, 27*(2), 1152–1163.

Wang, J., and Coffey, B. S. (1992), Board composition and corporate philanthropy. *Journal of Business Ethics, 11*(10), 771–778.

Wang, M., and Hussainey, K. (2013), Voluntary forward-looking statements driven by corporate governance and their value relevance. *Journal of Accounting and Public Policy, 32*(3), 26–49.

Wang, R., Zhou, S., and Wang, T. (2020), Corporate governance, integrated reporting and the use of credibility-enhancing mechanisms on integrated reports. *European Accounting Review, 29*(4), 631–663.

Webb, E. (2004), An examination of socially responsible firms' board structure. *Journal of Management and Governance, 8*(3), 255–277.

Williamson, O. E. (1985), *The economics institutions of capitalism.* New York: Free Press.

World Business Council for Sustainable Development (WBCSD) (2020), *Modernizing Governance – ESG challenges and recommendations for corporate directors.* Retrieved from https://www.wbcsd.org/Programs/Redefining-Value/Business-Decision-Making/Governance-and-Internal-Oversight/Resources/Modernizing-governance-key-recommendations-for-boards-to-ensure-business-resilience. Accessed on 1 September 2020.

Zhang, J. Q., Zhu, H., and Ding, H. B. (2013), Board composition and corporate social responsibility: An empirical investigation in the post Sarbanes-Oxley era. *Journal of Business Ethics, 114*(3), 381–392.

4 From theory to practice

Board characteristics,
financial performance, and
the adoption of integrated
reporting

Research design

As previously illustrated, although voluntary disclosure is today more and more relevant, it is the board that has the last word (Chen and Jaggi, 2000) in deciding which and how much information an organisation should disclose (Eng and Mak, 2003). The effective functioning of the board is determined by its composition (Mizruchi, 2004), which can influence company financial performance as well as the quantity and quality of voluntary disclosure, including the possible adoption of integrated reporting. The diversity of the board is defined as the disparity of the characteristics presented by its members (Robinson and Dechant, 1997). The composition of the board can be described in various terms, such as the members' value system, nationality, gender, professional background, or by the size of the board (Van der Walt et al., 2006; Kang et al., 2007).

In this chapter, an empirical analysis of the relationships between board characteristics on the one side, and company financial performance and the adoption of integrated reporting on the other side, is carried out through recurring to a two-stage statistical model. In the first step, a multivariate regression analysis is run to examine the association between the board's professional experience and financial performance. In the second step, a non-parametric multivariate permutation test is conducted to understand how the professional profiles of directors can influence the decision to uptake this innovative reporting tool. The results emerging from the two-stage empirical analysis are then discussed.

Hypothesis development

The choice of variables has not been addressed in a traditional way, i.e. by selecting variables typically used in the agency theory context, such as the size of the board, its age and gender proportion, the presence of outside vis-à-vis inside directors or others (Van der Walt et al., 2006; Kang et al., 2007: for further reference see Chapter 3).

In this analysis, it was decided to go deeper and further refine the distinction between Insiders and outsiders by investigating the professional background of each outside board member in terms of resources they can provide to the company. To do so, the board member classification developed by Hillman et al. (2000) in the context of the Resource-Dependence theory, drawn on Baysinger and Zardkoohi (1986), and then used also by Markarian and Parbonetti (2007) and Enache and Garcia-Meca (2019), was adopted. Members of the board were thus classified into four general categories, namely, *Insiders, Business Experts, Support Specialists,* and *Community Influentials.* As a consequence, four variables assuming the value between 0 and 1 were defined, where each variable represents the proportion of board members of a company that belongs to one specific category.

Insiders (Ins) are board members who are or have been employees of the company under investigation. They tend to have a profound knowledge of the company and its strategic orientation, and, thus, they provide the board with their specific experience and information of 'inside nature'. This category of board members is not unique to Resource-Dependence theory, but it has also been used in the context of Agency theory, and more specifically, to investigate the effectiveness of the monitoring function of boards and generally the linkages with firm performance. In this respect, Mace (1986) points out that Insiders, thanks to their in-depth knowledge about the organisation and its competitive environment, do embody a fundamental source of information for outside directors. This can be true also in situations where outside directors should evaluate investment decisions (Raheja, 2005), or when CEOs do not want to reveal their private information (Laux, 2006; Adams and Ferreira, 2007). The presence of Insiders on the board, even though recently added to it, can also represent a valuable choice in terms of CEO appointment (Hermalin and Weisbach, 1988). Drymiotes (2007) demonstrates how the presence of Insiders into the board can facilitate the monitoring process. Although Insiders are often seen as lacking independence in that they are supposed or expected to act in the best interest of the CEO, rather than in that of shareholders, he shows that the need to include them in the corporate governance mechanisms can arise endogenously. In fact, Insiders can ensure that the board can commit to a monitoring role and, thus, align shareholders' and managers' interests.

As to the influence of Insiders on firm performance, Klein (1998) shows that the presence of Insiders on finance and investment committees can positively influence performance, especially in terms of long-term investment decisions. Other studies have demonstrated that the existence of Insiders in the boardroom is or not significant in terms of profitability (Bhagat and Black, 2001 or equally significant as that of outside directors (Wagner III et al., 1998).

H1A: The presence of Insiders is positively associated with corporate financial performance

The presence of Insiders has demonstrated to be a key feature also in regard to accounting change and innovation. Using accounting conservatism as a proxy for resistance to change, it is possible to observe that academic literature offers mixed results. Ahmed and Duellman (2007) hold that the existence of this category of directors is negatively associated with conservatism, while outside directors have a positive influence. On the contrary, Burke and Logsdon (1996) affirm that managers might not want to incur in costs related to CSR disclosure as it may require time to recover them. Looking at the dynamics taking place in the boardroom, Nicholson et al. (2017) show that outsiders and Insiders do not always behave being pushed by opposite interests. Indeed, they can both act to balance control and, ultimately, collaborate. Considered the ambiguity of the results so far achieved, as well as the innovative connotation that can be associated with integrated reporting, the following hypothesis is formulated:

H1B: The presence of Insiders is negatively associated with the adoption of integrated reporting

According to Baysinger and Zardkoohi (1986) and Hillman et al. (2000), the category of outside directors which has been widely used in the Agency theory context tends to be quite myopic in capturing the different nuances that this role can assume. Hence, those authors propose a further refinement of outsiders into Business Experts, Support Specialists, and Community Influentials.

Business Experts (BE) are managers, senior officers, or directors who have worked or are still working in other for-profit organisations. They tend to have quite a strong expertise on competitive environments and strategies, decision-making, and problem-solving, even though not at a specialist level but at a general management one. They represent a communication channel among companies and also vis-à-vis the wider community of stakeholders. Therefore, they embody a sounding board for ideas. In this respect, they can provide organisational legitimacy to the company. Having experience of other companies operating in similar industries (Jones et al., 2008) allows Business Experts to understand better the risks and opportunities a company is facing (Dass et al., 2014; Wang et al., 2015), and to provide the organisation with strategic information, they being able to advise it in addition to monitoring it.

H2A: The presence of Business Experts is positively associated with corporate financial performance

Thanks to the knowledge and experience they might have acquired in other companies that could have already started their journey towards the adoption of integrated reporting, the following hypothesis is also adopted.

H2B: The presence of Business Experts is positively associated with the adoption of integrated reporting

Support Specialists (SS) are those who have specific expertise in a specialised industrial, scientific, or professional field, such as lawyers, scientists, and accountants. Accordingly, they differ from Business Experts in that they lack general management skills (Markarian and Parbonetti, 2007), but their key function relies on supporting the board with their set of specialised skills (Baysinger and Zardkoohi, 1986) that are not always internally available. They can improve the capacity building functions of companies (Markarian and Parbonetti, 2007) and have a wide range of connections. They may be professionals in capital markets and R&D in intensive industries, acting as decision supporters (Baysinger and Zardkoohi, 1986) and providing specialisations to the management of the company (Hillman et al., 2000; Jones et al., 2008). Their understanding of the sector and their competences can help them assess, and sustain decisions on, many aspects of financial reporting. Furthermore, Krishnan and Visvanathan (2008) claim that there is evidence that Support Specialists with legal experience benefit the businesses in which they operate. In this sense, they will provide companies with specific knowledge and skills, which can help evaluate the many aspects of the legal implications and improve the quality of information available to the board. Support Specialists also make available specialised connections and capabilities that generally facilitate companies' access to finance. In light of the above, the following assumption is devised:

H3A: The presence of Support Specialists is positively associated with corporate financial performance

Similarly to the presence of Business Experts, on the basis of the acquired specialistic knowledge that they have, another hypothesis can be put forward. Indeed, integrated reporting might be perceived as generating a unique reporting practice, though some of its characteristics and information can also be found in sustainability reports. Its adoption can entail a specialistic type of expertise, especially in its first year of implementation. Accordingly, the following hypothesis can be formulated:

H3B: The presence of Support Specialists is positively associated with the adoption of integrated reporting

The Community Influentials are non-executive/outside directors such as current or retired politicians, clergy members, and leaders of social organisations. They provide a valuable non-commercial perspective on the proposed company actions and strategies (Hillman et al., 2000), and have knowledge, experience and connections relevant to the organisation's external environment. Their expertise with the community is intended to help society avoid costly missteps when its actions could inadvertently conflict with the interests of those forces (Hillman et al., 2000). Political ties are significant in highly developed institutional settings (Cooper et al., 2010). Community Influentials can have beneficial effects in this respect. They can help the company to navigate an uncertain and complex environment by providing expertise in bureaucratic and legislative procedures (Goldman et al., 2009). They bring linkages to the company and with the company's competitive environment offer their experience on, and create connections to, groups and community organisations (Michelon and Parbonetti, 2012). As a result, they can give valuable non-commercial perspectives, provide legitimacy, protect stakeholder interests in board discussions, and monitor industry decisions.

Despite these characteristics, the choice has been not to include the variable referring to this fourth category in the model here utilised, but to focus instead on the above illustrated three board member categories that are more closely and effectively linked to professional business expertise.

In addition to the collected variables just described, three control variables have been used for the construction of the model, and they are board size (*Boardsize*), calculated as the number of directors sitting on the board in the year of the first implementation of integrated reporting; company size (*Size*), calculated as the logarithm of total assets; and the Industry Profile (*IND*), a dummy variable which assumes value 0 if a company belongs to the service sector and value 1 if a company belongs to the manufacturing industry, thus simplifying the categorisation adopted by Chan et al. (2014).

Sample selection

In order to run the first stage of the analysis, the sample selected includes only firms that started adopting integrated reporting in the period 2015–2019. The reason to focus on this time interval is twofold. First, this period is related to the two strategic phases that the IIRC has implemented, namely, the Breakthrough Phase (2015–2017), which was aimed to achieve a meaningful shift in the adoption of the International <IR> Framework, and the Momentum Phase (2018–2020), which had the objective to prepare the context for the global adoption of the <IR> Framework. Second, the choice of that time interval is motivated by the acute difficulty of effectively reconstructing the composition of pre-2015 company boards years. This is principally due to the fact that data have to be hand-collected as they are not available on databases with the needed level of granularity.

The organisations included in the sample have been selected through systematic research on the companies' website, starting from the list of reports provided by the <IR> Reporters section of the <IR> Examples Database of the International Integrated Reporting Council (IIRC – www.integratedreporting.org). For each of these companies, the first voluntarily produced integrated report was examined to control that it effectively corresponded to an integrated report. In this respect, the decision has been to retain only those documents that explicitly stated that they were following the International <IR> Framework. This sample selection phase resulted in the identification of 39 organisations worldwide, with the exception of South African companies that are required to prepare integrated reports when listed on Johannesburg Stock Exchange.

The sample was further refined by dropping those organisations with missing Datastream and Thomson Reuters Asset4 accounting data that are mainly those which are not listed. It was decided to analyse only listed companies for two reasons. First, within a small company, the leading force is not in the hands of the board of directors, but it is often concentrated in one person, who can be the managing director, the owner, the CEO, the CFO, etc. Second, listed companies have data which are publicly and periodically published, and which are easily accessible and available to carry out the research here planned.

This selection phase resulted in a final sample of 39 organisations across eight industries and 14 countries. The sample comprises firms from six different continents, with the larger proportion of integrated reports' 2015–2019 adopters coming from Europe (nearly 60% of companies selected) and mainly France. The industrials and the financial sector have the largest proportion of firms adopting integrated reports (44%), followed by utilities (18%) and technology (13%) (see Table 4.1).

This sample was then used to conduct the first phase of the empirical analysis, testing the relationship between board composition and

Table 4.1 Sample distribution by country and industry

Panel A: Distribution by country

Country	2015	2016	2017	2018	2019	Total
Australia	0	0	0	0	1	1
Belgium	0	1	0	0	0	1
Brazil	0	0	0	1	0	1
France	2	3	4	3	0	12
India	0	1	1	2	0	4
Italy	1	2	0	1	0	4
Japan	4	0	0	1	2	7
Netherlands	1	0	0	0	0	1
Norway	0	0	0	1	0	1
Philippines	0	1	0	0	0	1
Spain	0	1	0	0	0	1
Switzerland	0	1	1	0	0	2
Turkey	0	1	1	0	0	2
United States	1	0	0	0	0	1
Total	*9*	*11*	*7*	*9*	*3*	*39*

Panel B: Distribution by industry

ICB industry	2015	2016	2017	2018	2019	Total
Basic materials	–	–	–	–	–	–
Consumer goods	1	–	2	1	–	4
Consumer services	–	1	–	2	–	3
Financials	1	3	2	2	–	8
Health care	1	1	–	–	–	2
Industrials	3	3	1	1	1	9
Oil & gas	1	–	–	–	–	1
Technology	1	1	1	1	1	5
Telecommunications	–	–	–	–	–	–
Utilities	1	2	1	2	1	7
Total	*9*	*11*	*7*	*9*	*3*	*39*

characteristics and financial performance of companies adopting integrated reporting for the first time in the period 2015–2019.

To run the second stage of the investigation inherent in the relationship between board features and experience and the actual decision of adoption of integrated reporting, there was introduced a match-paired control sample that is composed of firms that do not adopt integrated reporting in the period 2015–2019. The second group of IR non-adopters (matching sample) has been formed on the basis of the following criteria: industry sector classification (based on the Industry Classification Benchmark-ICB system created by Dow Jones and FTSE); geographical region (same country); corporate size (based on the volume of assets). The final combined sample is thus composed by 78 international listed companies (see Appendix 1).

For each of the organisations included in one of the two samples (main and control), the board composition and the professional background of its members in the year of adoption of integrated reporting were examined. For example, the 2015 board of directors was analysed if the company chose to adopt the integrated report at the end of that year or early 2016. The related integrated reports was produced and released during the 2016 financial year, as a consequence, then, of the 2015 board decision. The choice to collect data in different years depending on the time of the decision of adopting integrated reporting is relevant to actually understand which attributes were most significant in deciding to implement this new reporting practice.

Data were hand-collected from the integrated reports (for <IR> adopters) and/or the annual reports or websites (for non-IR adopters) of each company. In particular, the biography of each board member was read, and individuals were classified accordingly.

This overall investigation resulted in classifying 898 profiles: 464 for group 1 (<IR> adopters), and 434 for group 2 (non-IR adopters). Subsequently, the percentage weight of the three board member categories here considered has been calculated for each company in proportion to the total number of the directors sitting on its board.

Statistical analysis

As a first stage of the empirical analysis, a multivariate logistic regression model to evaluate if and to what extent corporate governance characteristics can be associated with corporate financial performance has been run.

Applicating this model to our variables, we obtained the following system of equations:

$$\begin{cases} \text{INS} = \beta_{1,0} + \beta_{1,1}\text{BSIZE} + \beta_{1,2}\text{ROA} + \beta_{1,3}\text{LEVERAGE} + \beta_{1,4}\text{MKTVAL} + \\ \qquad \beta_{1,5}\text{SIZE} + \beta_{1,6}\text{IND} + \varepsilon_1 \\ \text{BUSEXP} = \beta_{2,0} + \beta_{2,1}\text{BSIZE} + \beta_{2,2}\text{ROA} + \beta_{2,3}\text{LEVERAGE} + \\ \qquad \beta_{2,4}\text{MKTVAL} + \beta_{2,5}\text{LOGTAS} + \beta_{2,6}\text{IND} + \varepsilon_2 \\ \text{SPEC} = \beta_{3,0} + \beta_{3,1}\text{BSIZE} + \beta_{3,2}\text{ROA} + \beta_{3,3}\text{LEVERAGE} + \\ \qquad \beta_{3,4}\text{MKTVAL} + \beta_{3,5}\text{LOGTAS} + \beta_{3,6}\text{IND} + \varepsilon_3 \end{cases}$$

INS = the proportion of Insiders sitting on the board

BUSEXP = the proportion of Business Experts sitting on the board

SPEC = the proportion of Support Specialists sitting on the board

BSIZE = the total number of directors sitting on the board in the year of implementation of an integrated report

ROA = earnings before interests and taxes on assets

LEVERAGE = total debt to total assets

Market-to-Book Value Ratio = market value of equity divided by book value of equity at fiscal year end

SIZE = logarithm of total assets

IND = a dummy variable which assumes value 0 if a company belongs to the service sector and value 1 if a company belongs to the manufacturing industry

The descriptive statistics for the variables of the model are presented in Table 4.2.

In the companies that have started implementing integrated reporting, the mean of Business Experts present in the board is equal to 42.4%, that of Insiders to 29.7%, while that of the Support Specialists to 20.1%. On average, then, Business Experts are the most represented group among board members, followed by Insiders and Support Specialists.

Table 4.2 Descriptive statistics

Variables	N	Mean	Median	Std. dev.	Min	p25	p75	Max
INS	39	0.297	0.200	0.255	0.000	0.118	0.333	0.833
BUSEXP	39	0.424	0.429	0.221	0.000	0.302	0.564	0.857
SPEC	39	0.201	0.200	0.152	0.000	0.091	0.302	0.583
BSIZE	39	0.119	0.110	0.036	0.060	0.095	0.140	0.220
ROA	39	5.050	3.860	4.066	0.310	2.175	6.830	15.330
LEVERAGE	39	51.32	22.43	111.092	0.200	7.750	42.700	681.25
MKTVAL	39	2.096	1.720	1.380	0.480	1.155	2.420	6.410
SIZE	39	5.021	4.812	1.099	2.848	4.319	5.610	8.468
IND	39	0.462	0.000	0.505	0.000	0.000	1.000	1.000

Source: Author's elaboration.

At first sight, these results can be linked to the fact that Business Experts, having already worked in and for other organisations, may have experienced the adoption of integrated reporting. Similarly, Insiders know about the organisation and, therefore, it might be easier for them to understand and leverage on the integrated thinking that lies at the heart of integrated reporting. Support Specialist might act as consultants, thanks to their specific knowledge and competences.

As for the economic, governance, and industry-independent variables utilised, i.e. Company Size, ROA, Leverage, Market-to-Book Value Ratio, Board Size and Industry Profile, the average ROA is 5.050, which means a high average level of profitability for the sample companies. The mean leverage is 51.32, indicating that more than half of the capital of the selected companies belongs to third parties. The average size of the sample companies is 5.021. The board of directors is composed of an average of 11.9 members. The Market-to-Book Value Ratio is 2.096 and the Industry Profile is 0.462, indicating a slightly lower proportion of companies belonging to manufacturing as compared to services.

Table 4.3 presents the results of the Pearson's correlation matrix among the variables used in the multivariate regression model described above. It is possible to note that the variables that show the highest correlation index with Insiders are size (as the logarithm of total assets), ROA, leverage, and Industry Profile. This fact may suggest in an anticipated way, the statistical significance of these four variables vis-à-vis the phenomenon investigated. As for Business Experts, size appears to be strongly, but negatively correlated, which may indicate a non-significant relationship between the two variables. Of course, these preliminary findings need to be further tested through a more sophisticated analysis that will be developed in the following section.

Table 4.3 Pearson correlation matrix

Explanatory variables	INS	BUSEXP	SPEC
BSIZE	−0.049	−0.162	0.084
ROA	0.238	−0.004	−0.194
LEVERAGE	0.244	−0.148	−0.176
MKTVAL	0.041	0.079	−0.050
SIZE	0.303	−0.262	0.000
IND	0.318	−0.180	0.019

Source: Author's elaboration.

Multivariate regression analysis' results

As mentioned above, the first stage of the analysis is aimed to understand whether and to what extent board characteristics can be associated with the economic and financial performance of companies adopting integrated reporting. By applying the system of equations mentioned above, the following results were obtained (Table 4.4).

Since the Market-to-Book Value Ratio (MKTVAL) has the less significant coefficient estimates and none of them is statistically significant, it has been removed from the model.

The new reduced model (without MKTVAL) is compared with the previous full model. The p-value of the Pillai's test is equal to 0.658, confirming that the null hypothesis, according to which the coefficients of MKTVAL are equal to zero, cannot be rejected (Table 4.5).

Interestingly, the results emerging from the second, reduced model show that concerning the Insiders, the regression coefficient estimates of ROA, leverage, and industry profile are still significant, but in a weaker form. In other words, when the variable Market-to-Book Value Ratio is eliminated from the model, also the importance of company's profitability, leverage, and industry profile, as predictors of the

Table 4.4 Results of the multivariate analysis examining the relationship between board characteristics and economic and financial performance (full model, *p*-values in brackets)

Explanatory variables	INS	BUSEXP	SPEC
Intercept	−0.487	1.033	0.336
	(0.088)*	(0.001)***	(0.105)
BSIZE	2.247	−2.329	−0.638
	(0.073)*	(0.063)*	(0.475)
ROA	0.038	−0.019	−0.016
	(0.006)***	(0.154)	(0.105)
LEVERAGE	0.001	−0.001	0.000
	(0.007)***	(0.113)	(0.130)
MKTVAL	−0.045	0.029	0.014
	(0.213)	(0.419)	(0.581)
SIZE	0.058	−0.045	0.002
	(0.108)	(0.207)	(0.948)
IND	0.168	−0.094	0.005
	(0.036)**	(0.231)	(0.929)
R-squared	0.409	0.216	0.115

*significant at 0.10, **significant at 0.05, ***significant at 0.01.
Source: Author's elaboration.

Table 4.5 Results of the multivariate analysis examining the relationship between board characteristics and economic and financial performance (reduced model, *p*-values in brackets)

Explanatory variables	INS	BUSEXP	SPEC
Intercept	−0.577 (0.040)**	1.091 (0.000)***	0.365 (0.067)
BSIZE	2.105 (0.093)*	−2.237 (0.070)*	−0.592 (0.500)
ROA	0.029 (0.013)**	−0.013 (0.233)	−0.013 (0.112)
LEVERAGE	0.001 (0.011)**	−0.001 (0.133)	0.000 (0.140)
SIZE	0.072 (0.036)**	−0.054 (0.106)	−0.003 (0.899)
IND	0.135 (0.073)*	−0.072 (0.322)	0.016 (0.764)
R-squared	0.379	0.200	0.106

*significant at 0.10, **significant at 0.05, ***significant at 0.01
Source: Author's elaboration.

proportion of Insiders, diminishes, implying that the significance for Insiders of accounting-derived measures becomes less relevant, because there is no consideration of the unaccounted intangible capital proxied by the Market-to-Book Value Ratio. The statistical significance of traditional performance measures that are linked to corporate accounting seems to decline in the eyes of investors when not considering the role of intangible capital that is not shown in financial statements. These findings also appear to suggest a certain level of systemic relationships amid the different performance measures, at least in the perspective of Insiders sitting on the board.

Possible problems related to multicollinearity have also been checked (Table 4.6). It can be observed that the correlations do not take large absolute values. Hence, multicollinearity does not seem to be an issue. This is confirmed by the Variance Inflation Factors (VIFs) because all the values are less than 5. Furthermore, the graphs of residuals, the assumptions about the errors of the multivariate regression model (normal distribution with null mean, uncorrelation and homoscedasticity), seem to be plausible (see Appendix 2).

In terms of results of the multivariate regression, it is possible to note that as far as the variable of *Insiders* is concerned, there is a positive and significant association with the majority of the considered variables, namely ROA, leverage, size, board size, and industry

Table 4.6 Matrix of correlations between explanatory variables and variance inflation factors (VIFs)

	BSIZE	ROA	LEVERAGE	MKTVAL	SIZE	IND
BSIZE	1.000	−0.470	−0.219	−0.201	−0.066	−0.046
ROA		1.000	−0.252	0.608	−0.162	0.249
LEVERAGE			1.000	−0.143	0.167	−0.171
MKTVAL				1.000	−0.322	0.374
SIZE					1.000	0.064
IND						1.000
VIF	1.561	2.305	1.308	1.985	1.215	1.248

Source: Author's elaboration.

profile. This appears to be consistent with previous studies, which have shown that the presence of these professional skills on the board can positively influence the performance of companies (Kiel and Nicholson, 2003; Drymiotes, 2007). To put it differently, Insiders, who are the members of the board, who are or have been employees of the company, and who can contribute to a considerable extent to make decisions about its strategic orientation, influence the investments and, therefore, company performance. The in-depth knowledge that they have on the organisation appears to be a fundamental asset in driving its business success. In the sample under study, this emerges from findings to be particularly true for those companies that have a bigger size and larger boards and that operate in industries that in general have a larger presence of intangibles (services) than tangibles (manufactured). These results are consistent with both the stewardship and Resource-Dependence theories. According to the former, Insiders represent the board member category that is supposed to lead to superior corporate performance as they are seen as those who do not act against shareholders, but that is interested in maximising profit. If Resource-Dependence theory is adopted as a conceptual lens, this is also true, as Insiders are those that can provide the board with a profound knowledge on the company.

As regards the dependent variable of Business Experts, the multivariate linear regression has found a significant but negative relationship with board size and no association with the other variables. It appears that the smaller the size of the board is, the highest is the proportion of members with this professional background. This result could be linked to the increased need for Business Experts in smaller boards to reach a level of knowledge and experience about the company's industry and the operating context. Moreover, the uncorrelation found for this board member category with firm performance is consistent with the findings of previous studies (Kiel and Nicholson, 2003) according to which the relationship between Business Experts/ outside directors and firm performance is dependent on the underlying theoretical viewpoint adopted. If the Agency view of the firm is assumed, results have indicated that we would expect a positive and significant association between these variables, in that outside directors are called on to protect the interests of shareholders.

The Support Specialists show no significant relationship with any of the investigated variables. This lack of statistical connection could be attributed to the professional background of this category of board members, which varies greatly depending on the type of sector in which a company runs its activities. To be true, this type of members of company boards are those who have specific expertise in a particular area, e.g. if a company operates in a mechanical sector, probably engineers specialised in that sector will be sitting on the board. Despite these members could be relevant for business success and understanding the opportunities and possible strategies of the company, their presence does not necessarily affect the performance of organisations adopting an integrated report.

Multivariate non-parametric permutation test

Thus far, the relationship between corporate governance characteristics and the financial performance of companies adopting integrated reporting have been examined. Now, the relationship that may exist between the knowledge and experience of the board members and the decision to implement integrated reporting as a new accountability tool for the company is investigated through a non-parametric methodology, i.e. the multivariate permutation test (Pesarin and Salmaso, 2010; Bonnini et al., 2014), owing to the low numerosity of the organisations composing the main sample.

The hypotheses under investigation are the following:

$$H_0 : \left[\text{INS}_1 \overset{d}{=} \text{INS}_2 \right] \bigcap \left[\text{BUSEXP}_1 \overset{d}{=} \text{BUSEXP}_2 \right] \bigcap \left[\text{SPEC}_1 \overset{d}{=} \text{SPEC}_2 \right]$$

$$H_1 : \left[\text{INS}_1 \overset{d}{\neq} \text{INS}_2 \right] \bigcup \left[\text{BUSEXP}_1 \overset{d}{\neq} \text{BUSEXP}_2 \right] \bigcup \left[\text{SPEC}_1 \overset{d}{\neq} \text{SPEC}_2 \right]$$

INS_j: proportion of Insiders in group j,
BUSEXP_j: proportion of Business Experts in group j,

SPEC$_j$: proportion of Support Specialists in group j,
with $j = 1 \rightarrow$ adoption of IR, and $j = 2 \rightarrow$ non adoption of IR

For each company in the main sample (group 1), the following has been considered:

i   the difference between the proportion of Insiders in the board of the company and that of Insiders in the board of the matched company in the control sample (group 2)

ii   the difference between the proportion of Business Experts in the board of the company and that of Business Experts in the board of the matched company in the control sample (group 2)

iii   the difference between the proportion of Support Specialists in the board of the company and that of Support Specialists in the board of the matched company in the control sample (group 2).

For the j-th company, the trivariate observation of the differences defined above (difference of the proportion of Insiders, Business Experts, and Support Specialists) is supposed to be a realisation of the trivariate random variable $Y_j = \left(\text{DINS}_j, \text{DBUSEXP}_j, \text{DSPEC}_j \right)'$. Accordingly, the following model has been assumed:

$$
\begin{pmatrix} DINS_j \\ DBUSEXP_j \\ DSPEC_j \end{pmatrix} = \begin{pmatrix} \delta_1 \\ \delta_2 \\ \delta_3 \end{pmatrix} + \begin{pmatrix} \varepsilon_{j1} \\ \varepsilon_{j2} \\ \varepsilon_{j3} \end{pmatrix}
$$

that can be denoted with the following matrix notation

$$Y_j = \delta + \varepsilon_j,$$

where Y_j is the random vector of the three response variables for the j-th company, δ the vector of constant parameters that represent the effects of the adoption of the integrated reporting on the proportion of Insiders, Business Experts, and Support Specialists, respectively, and ε_j is a random vector whose components have null mean and median, with $j = 1,2,...,39$.

The hypotheses of the problem can be denoted as follows:

$H_0 : \delta = 0$

$H_1 : \delta \neq 0$

In other words, under the null hypothesis, $\delta_1 = \delta_2 = \delta_3 = 0$ and, under the alternative hypothesis, at least one of the three parameters is not null. Under the null hypothesis, the assumption of exchangeability holds, and the sign of the response variables (proportion differences) can be either positive or negative with equal probability 0.5. A suitable choice for the test statistic of each partial test is the sample mean of the differences.

From the descriptive statistics of Table 4.7, it is possible to observe that the average presence of Support Specialists in the boards of companies belonging to the main sample (group 1) is higher than that in the matched companies of the control sample (group 2), while the opposite is on average true for the other two board member categories (Insiders and Business Experts). This first result of the non-parametric model seems then to suggest that Support Specialists may play an important, differential role in companies adopting integrated reporting.

The combined permutation test with the Fisher combination function has then been applied. The global p-value is equal to 0.001. Hence, there is strong evidence in favour of the alternative hypothesis that the board composition of the two groups (main and control) of companies is not equal.

In order to control the family-wise error rate for the multiplicity of the test and avoid the inflation of the significance level of the overall test, the p-values of the three partial tests are adjusted according to the Bonferroni-Holm rule (see Table 4.8).

Table 4.7 Descriptive statistics of the proportion differences between the treated group (companies that adopt integrated reporting) and the control group (companies that do not adopt integrated reporting)

	N	Mean	Median	Std. dev.	Min	p25	p75	Max
INS	39	−0.047	0.014	0.283	−0.929	−0.147	0.125	0.510
BUSEXP	39	−0.102	−0.133	0.311	−0.720	−0.298	0.078	0.583
SPEC	39	0.129	0.091	0.178	−0.433	0.000	0.262	0.500

Source: Author's elaboration.

Table 4.8 P-values of the partial tests

	INS	BUSEXP	SPEC
Unadjusted *p*-value	0.314	0.048	0.000
Adjusted *p*-value	0.314	0.096*	0.000***

*significant at 0.10, **significant at 0.05, ***significant at 0.01.
Source: Author's elaboration.

Hence, the significance of the global test can be mainly attributed to the partial test on the proportion of Support Specialists but, to a lesser extent, also to the percentage of Business Experts. In other words, the board composition of the two groups of companies is different principally for the proportion of Support Specialists.

The possibility of confounding effects due to the different composition of the two samples in respect to the financial and dimensional situation has been investigated by applying the propensity score approach (Rosenbaum and Rubin, 1983). A logistic regression analysis with the dummy variable denoting the belong-ness to the main sample (group 1) as the dependent variable has been performed. According to the output of this analysis, none of the explanatory variables affects the binary response. Accordingly, confounding effects due to these factors can be excluded, and the two samples are well-balanced and the associated results sound.

The possibility that the financial year could take the role of confounding factor has also been considered. Hence, we have stratified the dataset by distinguishing data relating to the annual periods before or of 2016 (period 1) and the annual periods after 2016 (period 2). Basically, the overall problem has been broken down into six partial testing problems (two periods multiplied for three response variables, i.e. the categories of board members considered). The final global p-value is still 0.001, this confirming again the robustness of the global test in respect to the strategy of decomposition of the problem into subtests. The partial p-values are reported in Table 4.9. As to the choice of 2016 as a time divide for the dataset, this is amenable to the fact that until 2017, i.e. the year in which the 2016 integrated reports were produced, the European Directive no. 95/2016 was not enforced in the Member States, this generating a level playing field between European and non-European companies as to the sustainability and integrated reporting. This situation, of course, has changed for 2017 integrated reports that have been produced in 2018, since the coming into force of the national laws implementing the above Directive created a different legal and operational context for the large listed companies of the European Union, which represent nearly 60% of the main sample analysed (see Table 4.1).

Thus, we have a clear confirmation that the significance of the above global test can be mainly attributed to the partial tests on the rate of Support Specialists in the companies of the main sample (group 1). This finding appears to be true for both the periods, but it is more marked for the most recent years (after 2016 integrated reports). In other words, the board composition of the two groups of companies

Table 4.9 P-values of the partial tests after stratification by financial year

	INS		BUSEXP		SPEC	
	≤2016	*>2016*	*≤2016*	*>2016*	*≤2016*	*>2016*
Unadjusted *p*-value	0.056	0.915	0.287	0.083	0.010	0.001
Adjusted *p*-value	0.223	0.915	0.573	0.248	0.050**	0.007***

*significant at 0.10, **significant at 0.05, ***significant at 0.01.
Source: Author's elaboration.

is different primarily due to the proportion of Support Specialists. This result is more evident in particular for the most recent years (i.e. after 2016). This could be amenable to the fact that, as previously mentioned, European companies in 2017 started to comply with the Non-Financial Reporting Directive and hence, this category of outside directors could be of support to the board also in this respect.

Conclusion

While the presence of Insiders and Business Experts has shown to be related to a positive performance by companies that adopt integrated reporting, when it comes to the *decision* to adopt this innovative reporting practice, it is the proportion of Support Specialist that is key, together with that of Business Experts, though to a lower extent. By providing specific knowledge, the Support Specialists become the agents of change in the accountability practices (Gray and Nowland, 2017; Ramón-Llorens et al., 2019). This finding is consistent with those previous studies which have found that consultants can act as "purifying actors" in introducing accounting change in organisations (Christensen and Skaerbaek, 2010). Not only consultants are those more able to foster innovative reporting practices at a country level, as it has been the case for Germany with the introduction of Wissensbilanz for SMEs (Girella and Zambon, 2013), but their role is fundamental also at a micro, organisational level (Chiucci and Giuliani, 2017) and even more when they enter company boardrooms. In this context, they do not have to be perceived as those who only pursue their own interests (Qu and Cooper, 2011), but Support Specialists are capable of sustaining and favouring the value creation process of the organisation and its communication (through integrated reporting) towards shareholders and stakeholders.

Similarly, Business Experts, by having a thorough knowledge about other organisations – that might have already adopted integrated reporting – and the industry in general, can advise the company on the opportunities that this reporting practice can offer. From the results of the non-parametric test, board Insiders seem to play only a (statistically) marginal role in pushing reporting innovation, perhaps because of a function played of preservation of the status quo.

Finally, from a theoretical perspective, the results obtained suggest the need for a more 'ecumenic' view when addressing conceptually the role of boards towards accountability innovation, such as integrated reporting. Indeed, the findings cannot be framed within one single theory, be it Agency, Stewardship, or the Resource-Dependence, but they appear to support a complementary view of these theoretical approaches. Directors in the boardroom seem to play different roles according to their expertise and backgrounds, which, on the whole, can 'satisfy' the underlying conceptual premises and logics of the three different frameworks. Indeed, Support Specialists, and to a lesser extent Business Experts, can play a distinctive function vis-à-vis accountability innovation that is consistent with the Resource-Dependence theory, while Insiders' role could be more aligned with the assumptions of the Stewardship theory. In addition, as shown in Table 4.2, the presence of outside directors accounts for about 70% of the total board members in the companies analysed, indicating their capacity to protect shareholders' interests as predicated by the Agency theory.

Bibliography

Adams, R. B., and Ferreira, D. (2007), A theory of friendly boards. *Journal of Finance*, *62*, 217–250.

Ahmed, A. S., and Duellman, S. (2007), Accounting conservatism and board of director characteristics: An empirical analysis. *Journal of Accounting and Economics*, *43*(2–3), 411–437.

Baysinger, B. D., and Zardkoohi, A. (1986), Technology, residual claimants, and corporate control. *Journal of Law, Economics, & Organization*, *2*(2), 339–349.

Bhagat, S., and Black, B. (2001), The non-correlation between board independence and long-term firm performance. *Journal of Corporate Law*, *27*, 231.

Bonnini, S., Corain, L., Marozzi, M., and Salmaso, L. (2014), Nonparametric hypothesis testing. Rank and permutation methods with applications. Chichester: R. Wiley.

Burke, L., and Logsdon, J. M. (1996), How corporate social responsibility pays off. *Long Range Planning*, *29*(4), 495–502.

Chan, M. C., Watson, J., and Woodliff, D. (2014), Corporate governance quality and CSR disclosures. *Journal of Business Ethics*, *125*(1), 59–73.

Chen, C. J., and Jaggi, B. (2000), Association between independent non-executive directors, family control and financial disclosures in Hong Kong. *Journal of Accounting and Public Policy*, *19*(4–5), 285–310.

Chiucchi, M. S., and Giuliani, M. (2017), Who's on stage? The roles of the project sponsor and of the project leader in IC reporting. *Electronic Journal of Knowledge Management, 15*(3), 183–193

Christensen, M., and Skærbæk, P. (2010), Consultancy outputs and the purification of accounting technologies. *Accounting, Organisations and Society, 35*(5), 524–545.

Cooper, M. J., Gulen, H., and Ovtchinnikov, A. V. (2010), Corporate political contributions and stock returns. *The Journal of Finance, 65*(2), 687–724.

Dass, N., Kini, O., Nanda, V., Onal, B., and Wang, J. (2014), Board expertise: Do directors from related industries help bridge the information gap?. *The Review of Financial Studies, 27*(5), 1533–1592.

Drymiotes, G. (2007), The monitoring role of insiders. *Journal of Accounting and Economics, 44*(3), 359–377.

Enache, L., and García-Meca, E. (2019), Board composition and accounting conservatism: The role of business experts, support specialist and community influential. *Australian Accounting Review, 29*(1), 252–265.

Eng, L. L., and Mak, Y. T. (2003), Corporate governance and voluntary disclosure. *Journal of Accounting and Public Policy, 22*(4), 325–345.

Girella, L. and Zambon, S. (2013), Regulating through the "Logic of Appropriateness" and the "Rhetoric of the Expert": The role of consultants in the case of intangibles reporting in Germany. *Financial reporting, 3–4*(35), 75–109.

Goldman, E., Rocholl, J., and So, J. (2009), Do politically connected boards affect firm value?. *The Review of Financial Studies, 22*(6), 2331–2360.

Gray, S., and Nowland, J. (2017), The diversity of expertise on corporate boards in Australia. *Accounting & Finance, 57*(2), 429–463.

Hermalin, B. E., and Weisbach, M. S. (1988), The determinants of board composition. *The RAND Journal of Economics, 19*(4), 589–606.

Hillman, A. J., Cannella, A. A., and Paetzold, R. L. (2000), The resource dependence role of corporate directors: Strategic adaptation of board composition in response to environmental change. *Journal of Management studies, 37*(2), 235–256.

Jones, C.D., Makri, M. and Gomez-Mejia, L.R. (2008), Affiliate directors and perceived risk bearing in publicly traded, family-controlled firms: The case of diversification. *Entrepreneurship Theory and Practice, 480*, 359–85.

Kang, H., Cheng, M., and Gray, S. J. (2007), Corporate governance and board composition: Diversity and independence of Australian boards. *Corporate Governance: An International Review, 15*(2), 194–207.

Kiel, G. C., and Nicholson, G. J. (2003), Board composition and corporate performance: How the Australian experience informs contrasting theories of corporate governance, *Corporate Governance: An International Review, 11*(3), 189–205.

Klein, A. (1998), Firm performance and board committee structure. *The Journal of Law and Economics, 41*(1), 275–304.

Krishnan, G. V., and Visvanathan, G. (2008), Does the SOX definition of an accounting expert matter? The association between audit committee directors' accounting expertise and accounting conservatism. *Contemporary Accounting Research*, *25*(3), 827–857.

Laux, V. (2006), Board independence and CEO turnover. Working paper, University of Texas.

Mace, M.L. (1986), *Directors: Myth and reality*. Boston, MA: Harvard Business School Press.

Markarian, G., and Parbonetti, A. (2007), Firm complexity and board of director composition. *Corporate Governance: An International Review*, *15*(6), 1224–1243.

Michelon, G., and Parbonetti, A. (2012), The effect of corporate governance on sustainability disclosure. *Journal of Management & Governance*, *16*(3), 477–509.

Mizruchi, M. S. (2004), Berle and Means revisited: The governance and power of large US corporations. *Theory and Society*, *33*(5), 579–617.

Nicholson, G., Pugliese, A., and Bezemer, P. J. (2017), Habitual accountability routines in the boardroom: How boards balance control and collaboration. *Accounting, Auditing & Accountability Journal*, *30*(2), 222–246.

Pesarin, F., and Salmaso, L. (2010), *Permutation tests for complex data: Theory, applications and software*. Chichester: Wiley.

Qu, S. Q., and Cooper, D. J. (2011), The role of inscriptions in producing a balanced scorecard. *Accounting, Organisations and Society*, *36*(6), 344–362.

Raheja, C. G. (2005), Determinants of board size and composition: A theory of corporate boards. *Journal of Financial and Quantitative Analysis*, *40*(2), 283–306.

Ramón-Llorens, M. C., García-Meca, E., and Pucheta-Martínez, M. C. (2019), The role of human and social board capital in driving CSR reporting. *Long Range Planning*, *52*(6), 101846.

Robinson, G., and Dechant, K. (1997), Building a business case for diversity. *Academy of Management Perspectives*, *11*(3), 21–31.

Rosenbaum, P. R., and Rubin, D. B. (1983), The central role of the propensity score in observational studies for causal effects. *Biometrika*, *70*(1), 41–55.

Van der Walt, N., Ingley, C., Shergill, G. S., and Townsend, A. (2006), Board configuration: are diverse boards better boards?. *Corporate Governance: The International Journal of Business in Society*, *6*(2), 129–147

Wagner III, J. A., Stimpert, J. L., and Fubara, E. I. (1998), Board composition and organisational performance: Two studies of insider/outsider effects. *Journal of Management Studies*, *35*(5), 655–677.

Wang, C., Xie, F., and Zhu, M. (2015), Industry expertise of independent directors and board monitoring. *Journal of Financial and Quantitative Analysis*, *50*(5), 929–962.

5 Boards, reporting, and long-term value creation

Towards an integrated view

Conclusions

This book aimed to start shedding light on the relationship between board composition and features, company financial performance, and the adoption of a new accountability form – i.e. integrated reporting – that has made its appearance around ten years ago. Integrated reporting is implemented by companies on an entirely voluntary way (except for South Africa) and is based on an international principles-based Framework.

This type of accountability vehicle is characterised by the fact that it considers not only financial capital as a resource, but also other five capitals available to an organisation, i.e. human, intellectual, natural, social and relationship and manufactured. This report seeks to give providers of financial capital as well as other stakeholders a 360-degree representation of a company's strategy, governance, performance, and future outlook through an overview that combines financial and non-financial resources.

The integrated report intends to demonstrate not only how value has been created in the past, but also how this value creation process can continue in the short, medium, and long terms. This form of reporting should be grounded on integrated thinking, which allows to plan strategies and evaluate performance employing a systemic view of the organisations.

The complexity of integrated reporting and the associated demand for resources that it requires to be implemented is remarkable. There are many aspects to consider, such as time, experts who help the company set up this report, costs, and the organisational fatigue related to its preparation. Hence, one may wonder why many companies all over the world spend time and resources in dealing with this report, since it is not mandatory, apart from South Africa (where the release of an integrated report is required by the King IV Corporate Governance Code to companies listed at the Johannesburg Stock Exchange). To put it differently, one might ask which are the most preeminent reasons that prompted companies to make this choice.

When considering the pervasive connection that integrated report has with company strategic aspects, capitals, and future, it is easy to detect that one of the key determinants to uptake this innovative form of disclosure is corporate governance. Indeed, the way companies are governed influences their direction of travel. Precisely in this sense, it is the board of directors that has the power to decide if and to what extent a company could adopt new reporting practices. It is the board that has the last word.

Accordingly, after delineating the core theoretical and practical aspects evidenced in the literature on voluntary information and integrated reporting (Chapter 1), the relationship between corporate governance and this new disclosure practice has been investigated by examining the different national Corporate Governance Codes that have started aligning to the principles of sustainability and integrated reporting (Chapter 2). Beginning with the South African case, it has been observed that, although there are different ways to approach integrated reporting, the adoption of a language relating to the importance of 'stakeholder relationships', 'risks and opportunities', and 'value creation' have represented for many Codes the way to do it.

A review of the academic and professional literature, and in particular of that investigating corporate governance and its interaction with various areas of disclosure (voluntary, CSR, intellectual capital, and integrated reporting), has shown that a homogeneous view has not been reached as yet on what are the critical determinants able to explain why a company might undertake a process of adoption of a new accountability tool such as integrated reporting.

More specifically, as a result of this literature review, two are the issues that still appear in need of a more profound and solid understanding. The first issue is the nexus between the financial health of companies adopting for the first time integrated reporting and their corporate governance and, in particular, the professional backgrounds of their boards. A better understanding of this aspect would be useful to shed light also on the "impression management assumption" put forward in the literature reviewed, that assumes a linkage between the adoption of this form of disclosure and a hypothetical difficult financial situation of the adopting companies. The second issue regards the correlation between the decision to implement integrated reporting by a company and the composition of its board and the associated professional backgrounds. The above two problems seem to be quite open in the literature and subject to different theoretical interpretations and empirical analyses.

In light of the above issues, an empirical analysis was undertaken to investigate the composition of the boards of directors concerning its association with corporate financial performance and the decision of companies to adopt integrated reporting for the first time as a disclosure form.

As for the analysis of the board of directors, many scholars have taken into consideration board features such as age, gender, size, CEO duality (if the Chairman and the CEO correspond to the same person), level of education, etc. Furthermore, researchers have relied on the general distinction between inside and outside directors, which is typical of the agency theory perspective. This study goes deeper by also investigating the professional background of each member of the boards of the companies selected.

The analysis conducted is based on a main sample of 39 companies that have all produced voluntarily an integrated report for the first time in the period 2015–2019 (thus no South African company was included in the sample), for a total of 464 board members' profiles analysed (plus other 434 profiles of the control sample). The data were hand-collected from the integrated reports available on the web for each company. The directors have been subsequently grouped into the four categories advanced by Hillman et al. (2000), namely, Insiders, Business Experts, Support Specialists, and Community Influentials. The Insiders are the employees or the former employees of the company considered; the Business Experts are the (retired or current) managers of other companies; the Support Specialists refer to people with an expertise in a specific area, such as lawyers, scientists, accountants, business consultants, etc.; and the Community Influentials relate to those individuals having an influence capacity on the community, such as politicians, ambassadors, social entrepreneurs, etc. However, it has been decided to include in the statistical analysis only those categories that might be strictly related to the presence of professional expertise pertaining to companies. Hence, the category 'Community Influential' has been dropped.

After classifying each board member in one of the three remaining categories, a two-stage statistical analysis has been carried out.

First, a multivariate regression has shown that as far as the category of Insiders is concerned, there is a positive and significant association with the accounting-derived metrics illustrating corporate financial performance (Return On Assets (ROA), Leverage) and the control variables 'Board Size' and 'Industry Profile'. This result seems to imply that those members of the board who are or were employees of the company and, thus having in-depth knowledge about it, tend to have a positive influence on its business achievements. As regards the Business Experts, the multivariate regression has found no positive and significant relationship with the accounting-based performance metrics, this implying that the existence of outside directors who also work in other companies does not necessarily benefit the company. The only significant but negative association that has been found for Business Experts is with board size: the larger the board is, the less is the proportion of this category of directors. This outcome could be amenable to the possible willingness of companies not to be exposed to the phenomenon of interlocking directorates. In other words, companies first adopting integrated reporting might be interested in demonstrating that a variegated range of actors provide their strategic direction. However, when reducing the size of the board, the presence of Business Experts becomes fundamental. The presence of Support Specialists is instead not correlated in any way with the corporate financial performance of companies adopting integrated reporting.

A multivariate permutation statistical test has been conducted to examine the relationship between boards' composition and professional characteristics, and the choice to implement this accountability device. Amid the insightful results, the presence of outside directors, and specifically of Support Specialists as well as Business Experts, has emerged as key for influencing the adoption of integrated reporting. This connection can be attributed to the features of both those board categories. In fact, these members of the boards tend to have both an expertise of a specific professional area and general management culture. In other words, the decision to implement integrated reporting appears to rely essentially on the existence in the boardroom of a certain level of professional knowledge, expertise, and understanding of this accountability tool. This result is further proof that more diversified boards with different characteristics in terms of role and professional skills can contribute in a decisive way – even though with different weights – to the choice of adopting integrated report in a company on a voluntary basis.

In summary, it can be pointed out that integrated reporting requires a significant level of professional expertise for being understood and, then, implemented. The emerging need for specialistic knowledge and experience in the boardroom in order to adopt integrated reporting could yield to the observation that this decision is likely not to be conceived as a greenwashing exercise. The results here obtained appear in

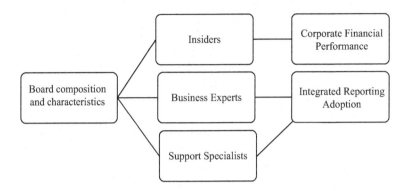

Figure 5.1 Empirical results.
Source: Authors' elaboration.

fact to show that such specialistic expertise increases the level of disclosure. Hence, in the company cases analysed, voluntary disclosure does not take symbolic forms (Hopwood, 2009; Cho et al., 2010). These outcomes are further confirmed by the analysis of the financial performance of those companies that have first adopted integrated reporting (Figure 5.1). In general, these organisations do not show particular criticalities from a financial performance perspective, as demonstrated also by the descriptive statistics of Table 4.7 in Chapter 4.

Therefore, the findings of this research seem to depart from those of previous studies that have conceived integrated reporting mainly as being a component of an impression management strategy embraced by managers to positively influence shareholders perceptions (Melloni et al., 2017).

From the analysis conducted in this study, it is possible to draw some more general conclusions. As repeatedly pointed out, in the last ten years, a new accountability means has made its appearance on the voluntary disclosure stage, i.e. integrated reporting.

• The role of boardrooms in adopting this innovative reporting practice can be hardly underestimated. Indeed, integrated reporting produces effects on strategic, managerial, organisational, and cultural aspects of company life, and this cannot be considered outside the boards' scope of attention and action. On the other hand, it can be observed that boards of companies of similar size, industry, and located in the same countries or regions may denote different attitudes towards integrated reporting.

- In general terms, these mindsets are likely to be amenable to the prevailing company culture and, in particular, its orientation towards transparency, accountability, and reporting innovation. The organisational inertia of a company, primarily represented by the Insider members of the boards, may constitute an obstructing factor to the taking up of a new reporting tool and culture.
- The general company attitude vis-à-vis integrated reporting seems then to be fundamentally linked to corporate governance and, more specifically, the culture instilled in the company by its board of directors and the cultural and professional orientation and experience of some of its members.
- However, the present research has revealed that the attitude of boards is a combination of all the different cultural approaches and professional backgrounds of the people composing those boards. In this respect, hence, if we want to understand better the decision of a company to uptake the innovative practice of integrated reporting, we should not only comprehend the general culture of a company, but also dig into the dynamic blend of the specific cultures of its board members. In other words, corporate boards should not be conceived as monolithic and unsegmented bodies, but as being articulated by many different souls.
- From a theoretical perspective, the analysis has shown that the confrontation between the three most relevant conceptual approaches regarding corporate governance (Agency, Stewardship, and Resource-Dependence theories), thus far competing in the arena of conceptual ideas for framing the role of corporate boards, may be to some extent overcome in the name of a wider and more integrated view of today role of boardrooms. The findings of this research appear to provide us with a more multifaceted vision of board functions that goes beyond the traditional understanding of boards as the mere watchdog of shareholders (Agency theory). The decision itself by the board to implement integrated reporting in a company shows its willingness to embrace a broader perspective with an evolutionary interpretation of its own role. This more proactive conceptual view of boards' work incorporates the need to take into account the information relationships also with other stakeholders and the osmosis with the external environment and its impinging factors (Resource-Dependence theory), while preserving – especially through Insiders, i.e. current or former company managers – a careful eye on the equilibrated development of the organisation in the short, medium, and long terms (Stewardship theory).

Policy implications, study limitations, and future research paths

From a policy perspective, most of the Corporate Governance Codes examined in Chapter 2 call for the presence of outside directors. However, the findings of this study have demonstrated that even more specific indications can be included in these Codes in terms of knowledge and expertise these actors could and should have, if a more transparent and a stakeholder attitude is to be thrusted in companies' boards in the near future.

The research does not lack some limitations, especially from a methodological perspective. The most relevant one is that the analysis has been conducted on a reduced number of observations, i.e. the companies (outside South Africa) that have started adopting integrated reporting in the period 2015–2019. Moreover, only the year of the first adoption of this reporting practice has been considered here, and not the following periods.

In this respect, the book also indicates some future research paths. First, a similar examination could be expanded in terms of both the number of 'first adopters' and years investigated. Actually, a longitudinal exercise could provide more insights into the role of the board of directors in promoting non-financial reporting innovation. As an example, a comparison of the composition of the board before and after this adoption could further enhance the advisory function of this crucial company body.

Second, the role of the board of directors in encouraging the adoption of integrated reporting could also be investigated in the context of other theories, beyond agency, stewardship, and Resource-Dependence approaches, if not through an integration of these theoretical frameworks.

An additional line of enquiry can be represented by further refinement of the disaggregation of the professional composition of the boards of directors of companies that have decided to adopt integrated reporting. This can be done by taking into consideration also the so-called 'grey directors', which are those who result from having linkages with the company through business deals and/or family relationships (Baysinger and Butler, 1985; Weisbach, 1988) and the 'community influentials' (Fernández-Gago et al., 2017). This phenomenon has demonstrated to be quite strong in countries and regions such as, e.g. India and Asia. The inclusion of the influence of the CEO could also represent a valuable addition (Jain and Jamali, 2016; Ramón-Llorens et al., 2019).

When trying to understand the role of the board in introducing new accountability practices, research and practitioners could aim to depart from the traditional view that shareholders and managers have necessarily to pursue different goals and that the only function of directors is that of monitoring and exerting a fiduciary duty for shareholders aimed at trying to align these diverse, almost competing, interests. Directors seem not only act as investor watchdogs, but their role can be more comprehensive and potentially include also their ability to provide a whole set of resources to the organisation, of both tangible and intangible nature. They can then act as 'guarantors and stabilisers', capable of reducing environmental uncertainty for the sake of *all* stakeholders, thus playing a guarantee function for all the internal and external categories of actors affecting and being affected by corporate activity.

After all, echoing the recent article by Margaret Blair (2020), Emerita Professor of Law at Vanderbilt Law School, "corporations are governance mechanisms, not shareholders toys" [...]

> The [corporations'] original function was to provide for the governance of joint enterprises, developments, and projects that require the participation of a variety of different types of investors and other participants, and are expected to provide benefits for many different customers, clients, and communities. All hope to gain some advantage from interacting with the corporation.

Bibliography

Baysinger, B. D., and Butler, H. N. (1985), Corporate governance and the board of directors: Performance effects of changes in board composition. *Journal of Law, Economics, & Organization*, *1*(1), 101–124.

Blair, M. (2020), *Corporations are governance mechanisms, not shareholder toys, premarket.* https://promarket.org/2020/09/29/corporations-governance-mechanisms-not-shareholder-toys-friedman/, 29 September. Accessed on 2 October 2020.

Fernández-Gago, R., Cabeza-García, L., and Nieto, M. (2018), Independent directors' background and CSR disclosure. *Corporate Social Responsibility and Environmental Management*, *25*(5), 991–1001.

Hopwood, A. G. (2009), Accounting and the environment. *Accounting, Organisations and Society*, *34*(3–4), 433–439.

Jain, T., and Jamali, D. (2016), Looking inside the black box: The effect of corporate governance on corporate social responsibility. *Corporate Governance: An International Review*, *24*(3), 253–273.

Melloni, G., Caglio, A., and Perego, P. (2017), Saying more with less? Disclosure conciseness, completeness and balance in Integrated Reports. *Journal of Accounting and Public Policy*, *36*(3), 220–238.

Ramón-Llorens, M. C., García-Meca, E., and Pucheta-Martínez, M. C. (2019), The role of human and social board capital in driving CSR reporting. *Long Range Planning*, *52*(6), 101846.

Weisbach, M. S. (1988), Outside directors and CEO turnover. *Journal of Financial Economics*, *20*, 431–460.

Appendix 1

List of organisations in the main sample and in the control sample

Main sample	Control sample
A2A	Edison Rsp
Abn Amro	Van Lanschot Kempen
Agl energy	Ausnet services
Atos	Dassault systemes
Axa	Cnp assurances
Ayala	Rockwell land
Bic	Maisons Du Monde
Capgemini	Alten
Clariant	EMS chemie
Cnim groupe	Aurea
Ely Lilly	Biogen Inc
Garanti bank	Akbank
Givaudan	Sika
Hitachi chemical	Shin-Etsu chemical
Iberdrola	Endesa
Ibiden	Meiko electronics
Icade	Unibail Rodamco we stapled units
Itausa	Banco Do Estado Do Rio Grande Do Sul B Pn
Jsw energy limited	Power grid corporation of India
Kering	LVMH
Kyocera	Nitto Kogyo
Lintec	Toda Kogyo
Mahindra & Mahidra	Ashok Leyland
Maruti Suzuki	Bajaj Auto
Mindtree	HEXAWARE TECHS
Mowi	Salmar
Poste Italiane	Astm
Sanofi	Virbac
Scsk	Itochu Techno-solutions
Snam	Saipem
Societe Generale	Bnp Paribas
Solvay	TESSENDERLO GROUP
Suez	Derichebourg
Thales	Safran

Main sample	Control sample
Toyota Tsusho	Marubeni
TS TECH Co.	NGK Spark Plug
Tskb	Sekerbank
Unipol	Cattolica Assicurazioni
Worldline	Euronext

Appendix 2
Analysis of residuals

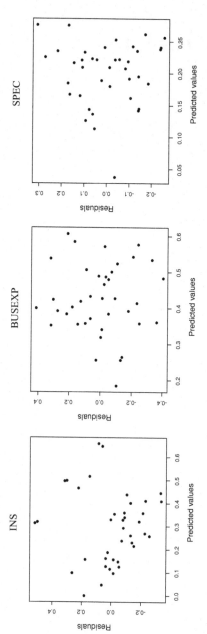

Figure A.1 Residuals versus predicted values.

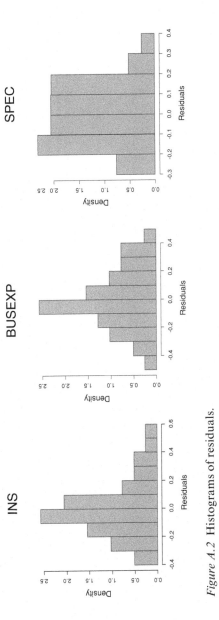

Figure A.2 Histograms of residuals.

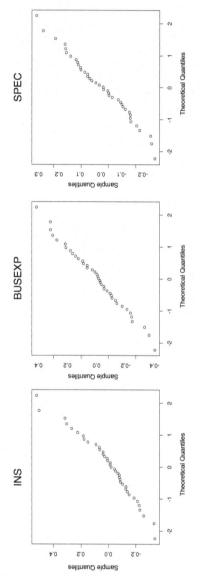

Figure A.3 Normal QQ-plot of residuals.

Index

Note: **Bold** page numbers refer to tables; *italic* page numbers refer to figures and page numbers followed by "n" denote endnotes.